Self Development with the Zodiac Oracle

Alan Butler

GW00633317

foulsham

LONDON • NEW YORK • TORONTO • SYDNEY

foulsham

Yeovil Road, Slough, Berkshire SL1 4JH

ISBN 0-572-01652-2

Copyright© 1992 Alan Butler

Printed in Great Britain by Cox and Wyman Ltd., Reading.

This book is dedicated to anyone who is troubled, perplexed or in need of a friend.

Contents

INTRODUCTION

The Zodiac Oracle is a very unusual book. It exists to give advice to people who are confused or troubled but it will also be of use to any individual who is interested in astrology or numerology.

The work hinges on one basic premise, that everything on the earth, material and spiritual, responds to the subtle influences of planetary movement and interaction. This belief has grown into the complex and fascinating subject of Astrology, an exacting craft whose origins are lost in the mists of time.

Sophisticated Astrological systems existed in the Babylonian and Egyptian eras. By early medieval times, the practice of Astrology had branched into three divisions: judicial astrology, which is the creation of individual horoscopes for interpretation, horory astrology, the art of interpreting a chart set for the moment of casting a question, in order to answer that question, and mundane astrology, which forecasts events of national importance.

Many people have had their personal birth charts, or horoscopes, cast by a reputable astrologer, and have discovered for themselves how accurate the subject can be in terms of character analysis, potential, future trends and spiritual growth. What very few individuals realise, surprisingly even devotees of the science, is that the influence of astrology doesn't end with human nature, in fact it was more likely to have been a desire to understand the world about them that encouraged early cultures to take an interest in the star clad heavens, rather than a desire to discover what lay in store for the individual within the group.

It stands to reason that if every object in the world is ruled, or perhaps more properly affected by, the stars and planets, there must be an intimate relationship between all such objects and arguably a link that exists on a spiritual, as well as the more easily understood physical plane. It is this subtle yet inextricable association between the component parts that make up creation which is utilised in the divination procedure and responses of the Zodiac Oracle.

The reader will discover in the next section how to obtain a response from the Zodiac Oracle, but individuals who are not serious adherents of Astrology may well still be puzzled why the book works in the way that it does. The short answer is that the Oracle works because the enquirer has a need that it should do so. In fact experience has proved that the greater the requirement of the user, the more sympathetic and accurate the response is likely to be.

To many this will be no satisfactory answer, yet oracles of all kinds have been consulted by mankind since time immemorial and have never diminished in popularity.

One might find a partial explanation in the theory of synchronicity, a word first coined by the famous Psychologist Carl Jung, who was a contemporary and originally a pupil of Sigmund Freud.

Jung speculated that there are inextricable links between all events, and the effects of a tiny minority of these we observe as apparent coincidences. Often such happenings string themselves together, forming the most complex and astounding patterns. These constitute the tip of a fantastic iceberg that appears in the conscious world, but is in fact only a tiny part of the synchronicity that we might observe on a subconscious level.

It might be argued that an esoteric work such as the Zodiac Oracle defies any logical explanation, though today's world demands that we try to understand the ins and outs of all happenings. It could be further postulated that The Zodiac Oracle only puts us in touch with what we already know anyway on a subconscious level. Whatever the answer may be, there are hundreds of testimonies of ways in which this work has assisted people to discover more about themselves and the workings of their innermost minds.

It must be stated from the outset that the Oracle will not work for everyone immediately, and again there is no definitive explanation for why this should be so. Some readers will find an affinity with its format and purpose at once, whilst for others it will take time and practice to understand what message the Oracle is seeking to impart. One fact is certain however. No person who is genuinely open minded or in need of a friend will be disappointed.

About The ZODIAC ORACLE

The Zodiac Oracle is composed of three hundred and sixty responses. These are short stories, or fables, and have been carefully constructed in such a way that each of them responds to a specific degree of the zodiac wheel.

At the beginning of the book you will find outlined the procedure for divination. Readers will be able to consult the Oracle, about any question or problem that may be on their mind. The divination procedure is based on Cabbalistic Numerology and has been specifically designed so that, through a series of simple conversion tables, the name of the questioner, together with the time and date of the enquiry, will lead to a particular sign and degree of the zodiac. The Oracle will not necessarily provide the answer that the reader expects but the one most relevant to the question. Some short meditation on the response may initially be necessary, though the Oracle often works with such startling clarity that the questioner should be left in no doubt as to the meaning and significance of the response.

When turning to the relevant zodiac sign, the reader will first come across a short passage related to the characteristics of that segment of the zodiac, this forms the first part of the Oracle's response. When the sign degree is consulted the prime response is a short story or statement, this being the second and major part of the Oracle's response to any given enquiry. Several words follow the degree response, the first is the 'Keyword'. Second is the word 'Element', followed by the elemental rulership of the sign in question, for example 'Fire'. Explanations of the four elements can be found at the back of the the Oracle. Some readers may find these useful when interpreting responses. (See pp 157 - 60). Finally there is the word 'Planet', followed by the name of the planet associated in classical astrology with the sign in question, for example 'Mars'. At the back of the book is an explanation of the planets and their functions in astrological rulership. The reader may find that this explanation is also helpful in answering the original enquiry. (See pp 148 - 56). The single 'Keyword' might be useful as a quick reference to the Oracle's response to any given question, though the reader must understand that for a holistic and accurate understanding of the Zodiac Oracle's response, the various passages should be read and considered in full and carefully.

How To Use
THE ORACLE

U sing the system of Cabbalistic numerology necessary to consult the Oracle is really very simple. All you will need is a pen and a piece of paper. Almost any sort of question is relevant, provided it is asked with a genuine need, though the responses that you sometimes receive may surprise you and could even answer a more fundamental question than the one you originally asked.

First of all it is very important to visualise inwardly the question or problem that is uppermost in your mind. Keep the enquiry as simple as possible because if you visualise a compound question the response you receive might not be too easy to understand.

See if you can find a quiet spot to consult the Oracle, away from noise or possible interruptions. If there are too many distractions your concentration will be affected, making it difficult for you to hold the visualisation in your mind. Once you have meditated for a moment or two on your question or problem, take the pen and paper and write your name down the left hand column as shown below. Use the name that you are usually known by if it is different from your full name. Below is an example name and the way that you should list it on the paper.

J
O
H
N

S
M
I
T
H

Now turn to Table A, on page 13. Here you will find a list of phonetic sounds and their Cabbalistic corresponding number values. Becoming accustomed to using the phonetic table will take a short while but you will soon find it quite easy.

Take the sounds of your name, break them down into phonetic

components and write the corresponding number value against the letter, or group of letters in question. Let me demonstrate with the example.

J is in the line I - Y - J - Ee and has a number value of 10, so against J we write down the number 10.

J = 10

The sound O has a value is 16, so we write that down beside the letter O in John.

O = 16

In the name John the letter H is not sounded at all verbally so we miss it out. The next letter N is valued at 14 and this is the number that we jot down beside it.

Continue in this way until you arrive at the end of the name. In the example the finished list would be as follows.

J = 10
0 = 16
H = 0
N = 14

S = 21
M = 13
I = 10
TH = 9

To the bottom of this list you now need to add the time of asking the question, breaking this down into hours and minutes. Use the twelve hour clock, so that if our example was asked at half past ten in the evening, the list would now look as follows.

J = 10 O = 16 H = 0 N = 14

S = 21
M = 13
I = 10
TH = 9
10
30

Now add the numbers together as you would with simple arithmetic. In the case of the example the resultant figure is 133. Remembering the number, now turn to table B. Somewhere in the right hand columns you will find the number in question. When you have located it, trace back to the left in the same column until you arrive at the name of a zodiac sign. This is the sign that your answer lies in. In the case of the example the sign would be Pisces.

To obtain the degree of the sign that forms the answer to your question a similar procedure is followed but this time instead of using your name it is the date on which the question is asked that is utilised. If in our example the date was October 3rd 1992 we would list it as follows.

3
10
1
9
9
2

To the bottom of this list we once again have to add the time. The clock will usually have moved on a minute or two while you were carrying out your original calculations so in the example we will assume that the time is now thirty two minutes past ten. The list now looks like this.

3
10
1
9
9
2

10
32

Once again add the numbers together and this time refer your answer to Table C. Look at the right hand columns to find your number and then trace across to the left side to discover the degree of the sign that contains the response relating to your enquiry. The example adds up to 76 and so the degree of Pisces where the relevant advice could be found would be 23'.

You now have several responses to read. The first is the Zodiac sign description. This will often reflect the attitude that you take towards your enquiry. Next comes the main response, ie. the short story occupying the zodiac degree that you have arrived at. This should be the solution or advice that you are seeking, though remember it might take some thought before you respond fully to its significance.

For further verification you can look at the keyword, and also the element ruler and planet ruler, mentioned in the previous section.

A word of caution. The Zodiac Oracle was never meant to be a party game and in its own gentle way it might rebuke you if you use it as such. Concentration on your real problems and a reverence for the timeless methods that the Oracle uses should lead you to the answers you need, though not necessarily the ones you expected. Use the Oracle with care and it will not let you down.

TABLE A

NUMBER	SOUND
1	A-Ah-Aa
2	B
3	G
4	D
5	E-Eh-Ay
6	U-V-W-Oo
7	Z
8	H-Ch
9	Th
10	I-Y-J-Ee
11	C-K-Ck
12	L
13	M
14	N
15	X
16	O-Oh
17	F-P-Ph
18	Sh-Ts-Tz
19	Q
20	R
21	S
22	T

TABLE B

Sign																													
ARIES	1	24	25	48	49	72	73	96	97	120	121	144	145	168	169	192	193	216	217	240	241	264	265	288	289	312	313	336	337	360
TAURUS	2	23	26	47	50	71	74	95	98	119	122	143	146	167	170	191	194	215	218	239	242	263	266	287	290	311	314	335	338	359
GEMINI	3	22	27	46	51	70	75	94	99	118	123	142	147	166	171	190	195	214	219	238	243	262	267	286	291	310	315	334	339	358
CANCER	4	21	28	45	52	69	76	93	100	117	124	141	148	165	172	189	196	213	220	237	244	261	268	285	292	309	316	333	340	357
LEO	5	20	29	44	53	68	77	92	101	116	125	140	149	164	173	188	197	212	221	236	245	260	269	284	293	308	317	332	341	356
VIRGO	6	19	30	43	54	67	78	91	102	115	126	139	150	163	174	187	198	211	222	235	246	259	270	283	294	307	318	331	342	355
LIBRA	7	18	31	42	55	66	79	90	103	114	127	138	151	162	175	186	199	210	223	234	247	258	271	282	295	306	319	330	343	354
SCORPIO	8	17	32	41	56	65	80	89	104	113	128	137	152	161	176	185	200	209	224	233	248	257	272	281	296	305	320	329	344	353
SAGITTARIUS	9	16	33	40	57	64	81	88	105	112	129	136	153	160	177	184	201	208	225	232	249	256	273	280	297	304	321	328	345	352
CAPRICORN	10	15	34	39	58	63	82	87	106	111	130	135	154	159	178	183	202	207	226	231	250	255	274	279	298	303	322	327	346	351
AQUARIUS	11	14	35	38	59	62	83	86	107	110	131	134	155	158	179	182	203	206	227	230	251	254	275	278	299	302	323	326	347	350
PISCES	12	13	36	37	60	61	84	85	108	109	132	133	156	157	180	181	204	205	228	229	252	253	276	277	300	301	324	325	348	349

TABLE C

1°	29	31	89	91	149	151	209	211	269	271	329	331
2°	27	33	87	93	147	153	207	213	267	273	327	333
3°	25	35	85	95	145	155	205	215	265	275	325	335
4°	23	37	83	97	143	157	203	217	263	277	323	337
5°	21	39	81	99	141	159	201	219	261	279	321	339
6°	19	41	79	101	139	161	199	221	259	281	319	341
7°	17	43	77	103	137	163	197	223	257	283	317	343
8°	15	45	75	105	135	165	195	225	255	285	315	345
9°	13	47	73	107	133	167	193	227	253	287	313	347
10°	11	49	71	109	131	169	191	229	251	289	311	349
11°	9	51	69	111	129	171	189	231	249	291	309	351
12°	7	53	67	113	127	173	187	233	247	293	307	353
13°	5	55	65	115	125	175	185	235	245	295	305	355
14°	3	57	63	117	123	177	183	237	243	297	303	357
15°	1	59	61	119	121	179	181	239	241	299	301	359
16°	2	60	62	120	122	180	182	240	242	300	302	360
17°	4	58	64	118	124	178	184	238	244	298	304	358
18°	6	56	66	116	126	176	186	236	246	296	306	356
19°	8	54	68	114	128	174	188	234	248	294	308	354
20°	10	52	70	112	130	172	190	232	250	292	310	352
21°	12	50	72	110	132	170	192	230	252	290	312	350
22°	14	48	74	108	134	168	194	228	254	288	314	348
23°	16	46	76	106	136	166	196	226	256	286	316	346
24°	18	44	78	104	138	164	198	224	258	284	318	344
25°	20	42	80	102	140	162	200	222	260	282	320	342
26°	22	40	82	100	142	160	202	220	262	280	322	340
27°	24	38	84	98	144	158	204	218	264	278	324	338
28°	26	36	86	96	146	156	206	216	266	276	326	336
29°	28	34	88	94	148	154	208	214	268	274	328	334
30°	30	32	90	92	150	152	210	212	270	272	330	332

♈

ARIES

Out of the chaos comes order.
In the midst of the void a pattern is discernible.
Within this pattern, consciousness is born
and the spring of human spiritual endeavour
can flow around the Earth
and out into the boundless universe
beyond.

Degree 1

The machine-gun's rattle is at last silent and in the squalor and filth of the trench the soldier now has time to write a letter. In the communication he talks of the joys of summer and the warmth of a remembered embrace. Meanwhile, the rats run and scamper unconcerned around his feet in the mud.

Keyword RESPITE

Element Fire
Planet Mars

Degree 2

Despite the fact that he is employed to prevent theft, the store detective has for two years watched a particularly frail old lady deposit a small packet of tea into her shopping bag on the same day each week. Feeling himself powerless to prevent this occurrence, the detective is ruthless in his vigilance on every other occasion.

Keyword COMPASSION

Element Fire
Planet Mars

Degree 3

The arrival of the lamb is perhaps the first true herald of spring and on what seems like the coldest of days, when a frost still clings to the grass and snow lies heavy on the hills, the new lambs are there, a certain sign that the first flowers of nature's revival will soon bedeck the hedgerows.

Keyword HOPE

Element Fire
Planet Mars

17

Degree 4

The Smithy is warm and the bellows busy as the burly black-smith works with his hammer and hot iron at the anvil. The horseshoe that he is creating is identical with, though uniquely different from, every other that he has manufactured in his long career. The blacksmith knows this, though his apprentice, who pumps the bellows, is bored with the monotony of his routine.

Keyword ORIGINALITY

Element Fire   *Planet* Mars

Degree 5

A certain old countryman is proud of his ability to trap the rabbits in his district and because of his skill and experience no other local can better his exploits. Late one Spring the countryman walks to his allotment, intent on picking succulent spring greens for his dinner. Upon arriving at the plot, he discovers that his entire crop has been eaten by rabbits.

Keyword RETURN

Element Fire   *Planet* Mars

Degree 6

Rooks are notorious for being ragged and untidy birds and are often marked as thieves. Though intelligent, their numbers have been kept low by farmers whose first aim is to protect their crops. For centuries, however, experienced folklorists have marked the possible heat of the coming summer by noting at what height in the trees the rooks build their nests.

Keyword OBSERVATION

Element Fire   *Planet* Mars

Degree 7

Filled with aggression, an angry child smashes her toys in a frenzy of frustration. She is not aware that her future pleasure may be marred by her present state, for in the depths of anger or sorrow there is no tomorrow. Later the aggression will be forgotten but the toys will still be broken.

Keyword FAR-SIGHTEDNESS

Element Fire *Planet* Mars

Degree 8

Speaking in purely human terms, Hyenas are a cowardly species. Waiting on the periphery of a kill until the lion or other predator wanders off, they then dash in to salvage the remnants. Despite their apparent cowardice however, hyenas possess jaws capable of smashing the largest of bones as if they were matches.

Keyword CONTROL

Element Fire *Planet* Mars

Degree 9

At the end of a busy and fairly lucrative day, the onion seller prepares to return to his home for a well earned rest. Before doing so he visits a gentlemen's cloakroom in the town to change his clothes. When he emerges, his beret and french accent have mysteriously disappeared and now, like most of his neighbours, he carries an umbrella and a briefcase.

Keyword DECEPTION

Element Fire *Planet* Mars

Degree 10

Few people notice the elderly businessman who throws bread to the wildfowl in the park lake. To most passers-by he is a nondescript character and has no tangible effect on their lives. Three or four generations of birds however have viewed him as being god and provider, for winter and summer alike he is always there. On one level he is invisible whilst on another he is revered.

Keyword UNDERESTIMATION

Element Fire   *Planet* Mars

Degree 11

Stoking a greedy furnace, the attendant workers are parched by the searing heat. As they sweat at their toil, above in the bath house a merchant, seeking relief from the pressures of the day sits and perspires in happy relaxation in the steam room that the furnace supplies with heat.

Keyword DEGREE

Element Fire   *Planet* Sun

Degree 12

Before the returning soldier the long road stretches ahead. Such a distance would have seemed much shorter with victory to spur him on but in the face of defeat he is feeling every mile. Hanging dead on the barbed wire back at the battle-field is another soldier who's army was victorious.

Keyword ALTERNATIVES

Element Fire   *Planet* Sun

Degree 13

The planet Mars is a cold and inhospitable world with a thin and poisonous atmosphere and little of apparent benefit when viewed in comparison with our own planet. It may however be rich in precious minerals and the sight of red Mars, when viewed from the Earth is one of the most beautiful spectacles in the sky.

Keyword OBSCURATION

Element Fire   *Planet* Sun

Degree 14

At the moment that his opponent is wavering slightly and obviously groggy, the prize fighter fails to attack as strongly as he should and as a result subsequently loses the contest. When questioned later as to why he hesitated, the seasoned pugilist replies that he sensed that his opponent tonight could not stand the humiliation of defeat.

Keyword COMPASSION

Element Fire   *Planet* Sun

Degree 15

In the witness box of a court room a woman defends her lover who is the accused. She declares him incapable of the brutality with which he is charged. Although she is aware that she is committing perjury, the woman is equally certain that the statement she is making is true, at least from her own experience.

Keyword BLINDNESS

Element Fire   *Planet* Sun

Degree 16

Hhigh above the valley a ram stands on a rocky outcrop surveying his flock close by. In his horns he has had sufficient power to fight his way to the top of the pecking order and still has tenacity enough to maintain his position. When he is confronted by potentially harmless mountaineers, despite his strength and endurance, together with the rest of his herd, weak and strong alike, he flees to safety.

Keyword RECOGNITION

Element Fire   *Planet* Sun

Degree 17

Whilst plundering a house a certain burglar is disturbed by the occupant who is armed with a shotgun. The thief does not put up a struggle and is delivered into the hands of the police. In the end not only is the burglar arrested but also the house owner, for possessing a shotgun without a licence.

Keyword APPORTIONING

Element Fire   *Planet* Sun

Degree 18

Intent upon a well tried line of patter, the door-to-door vacuum cleaner salesman spends twenty minutes extolling the virtues of his product to a housewife. Again and again she tries to explain to him that she has no need of his machine but the salesman carries on all the same. Eventually she invites the persistent individual into her house, where he is shown that there are no electric power points from which to run the machine.

Keyword OBSERVATION

Element Fire   *Planet* Sun

Degree 19

Expertly the fire eater transfers a flame from a fiery brand to his mouth and back to the brand again. Those in the audience marvel at his skill and ability to manipulate so dangerous a medium. One night the performer returns home after the show to find that during his absence a fire has broken out and burned his house down.

Keyword FAMILIARITY

Element Fire   *Planet* Sun

Degree 20

On a street corner a young woman stands collecting information for an advertising company promoting a new product. After a while she notices that the general reaction to the merchandise is not favourable, though many people admit to using it. A year later the opinions of most people are no more favourable, though the product is still selling well.

Keyword FICKLE

Element Fire   *Planet* Sun

Degree 21

An apprentice tries hard to copy a complex joint being cut by the master carpenter. After much perseverance, he manages to replicate the joint, though it is ill fitting and misshapen. The carpenter explains that when the apprentice starts to visualise the chair that he is making, the joint itself becomes easy to create

Keyword HOLISM

Element Fire   *Planet* Jupiter

Degree 22

In spite of his tremendous size and seemingly awkward gait a bear rarely goes hungry and is skilled in many different techniques for satisfying its appetite. Although it can survive alone in a harsh world it is not beyond plundering easy pickings if they lie within its reach. The bear will even steal from the habitation of man, its only natural enemy, if circumstances allow.

Keyword ADAPTABILITY

Element Fire   *Planet* Jupiter

Degree 23

An elderly and bedraggled lady is arrested for vagrancy because she is caught scavenging in a dustbin. When she receives only a caution she is flabbergasted. Being questioned afterwards as to why she was surprised at the verdict she explains that she expected to go to prison because the dustbin was that of a wealthy family.

Keyword PERSPECTIVE

Element Fire   *Planet* Jupiter

Degree 24

In legend the wolf stands alone as the archetype villain and pack hunter. He has been maligned and chased out of many countries where the species once flourished. The wolf's value ecologically was in culling sick and old animals from large herds, thereby keeping the strain pure, though for all his skills at hunting over vast distances and in spite of his awesome reputation a great percentage of the average wolf's diet is humble mice.

Keyword FLEXIBILITY

Element Fire   *Planet* Jupiter

Degree 25

Arriving at a building site one day a contractor discovers that vandals have wrecked some of his equipment during the night. Because of this eventuality he is forced to lay off some of his workers temporarily. One of the labourers returns home unaware that included amongst the vandals was his own son.

Keyword REPERCUSSIONS

Element Fire   *Planet* Jupiter

Degree 26

High on a lofty perch the regal and patient eagle surveys the countryside below. Barely a creature moves, no matter how small or distant, that is not observed by the eagle perched above. Each grass snake and vole is seen through the long hours of silent vigilance, though only rarely does the great bird leave its perch to dive for food. When it does so it is invariably successful.

Keyword PATIENCE

Element Fire   *Planet* Jupiter

Degree 27

A case of rifles is captured by a tribe of bushmen, but never having seen such devices before, only folk tales exist to speak of the power of the guns. They know the objects to have powerful magic but after trying the rifles as clubs and cudgels, breaking several in the attempt, they contemptuously throw them away and return to their accustomed spears.

Keyword IGNORANCE

Element Fire   *Planet* Jupiter

Degree 28

A certain car salesman is expert at selling the model of car for which he is responsible, having memorised all its technical specifications and being in any case a naturally good talker. Prospective customers cannot see the salesman's own car at the rear of the building, a different model altogether.

Keyword CONCENTRATION

Element Fire   *Planet* Jupiter

Degree 29

Two people argue. The basis of their disagreement is that a bus has just passed with only one seat available and both individuals claim to have been first in the queue. Whilst they stand and bandy words three almost empty buses come and go.

Keyword OBSTINACY

Element Fire   *Planet* Jupiter

Degree 30

When a competition winner discovers that the prize to which he is entitled is inferior to that which has been promised he is furious. In his anger he fails to realise that only a few hours previously he never even seriously considered the possibility of winning.

Keyword GRATITUDE

Element Fire   *Planet* Jupiter

ZODIAC SIGN 2

TAURUS

A mighty river flows between the known and the unknown. Some say the ferryman demands a fee. But every journey must commence, and to those who genuinely trust, the cost is an irrelevant detail. If the quest is imperative there will be no significant obstacles.

Degree 1

As the talented artist deftly puts the finishing touches to his latest portrait he scrutinises the canvas and then stares at the attractive model who has been sitting for him. Without a sigh or any sign of frustration the artist destroys the canvas and dismisses his model. She is perplexed but satisfied enough that she has been paid. The artist considers the money well spent.

Keyword CONTINUATION

Element Earth   *Planet* Venus

Degree 2

If treated gently and in a favourable mood, an often wild and ferocious bull can be led around by the farm children. However, should the bull be ill used or prevented from following his chosen path, the strongest farmhands have difficulty in controlling him.

Keyword RESERVE

Element Earth   *Planet* Venus

Degree 3

Paying their entrance fee, the queue of men quickly pass through the turnstile and on into the strip club of a red light district. Amongst the group are individuals who have been coerced by their companions into visiting the spectacle. Their reaction may well be one of boredom or revulsion, but would they admit the fact?

Keyword ACQUIESCENCE

Element Earth   *Planet* Venus

Degree 4

There is no permanence about the artistic creations that a hairdresser is responsible for making, no matter how talented the person concerned may be. The natural processes of hair growth are certain to win through in the end and then the client will be forced to return to the hairdresser once more for a temporary suspension of a time-ruled event.

Keyword EVOLUTION

Element Earth   *Planet* Venus

Degree 5

Working for a large estate, a gardener views with satisfaction the fresh new blooms of spring that, thanks to his constant care and attention, grow in neat order within the walls of the garden. Beyond the perimeters of the gardener's kingdom in the tangle of vegetation at the far side of the wall, the colours are just as bright, the scent as strong and the number of species greater.

Keyword ENDEAVOUR

Element Earth   *Planet* Venus

Degree 6

During the early part of the 1950's, the rabbit population of Western Europe was virtually decimated by myxomatosis, introduced to control the rabbits' numbers. Despite the scourge, such is the resilience of the species, that it has now recovered and, much to the alarm of farmers, is breeding as prolifically as ever.

Keyword RESILIENCE

Element Earth   *Planet* Venus

Degree 7

Members of an orchestra that is world famous are touring in a foreign country. One day a number of instruments are stolen whilst in transit. A double bass player, who has always been teased because of his bulky and awkward instrument, is relieved to find that his bass was too large for the thieves to tackle, though smaller instruments of greater value may never be recovered.

Keyword EVENTUALITY

Element Earth   *Planet* Venus

Degree 8

A poet who has recently visited a location of outstanding natural beauty completes a work dedicated to his personal appreciation of the scene. Future readers of the work may never have the chance to stand where the poet himself did, but in any geographical location can relive the creator's emotions.

Keyword INSPIRATION

Element Earth   *Planet* Venus

Degree 9

A vegetable stall in a busy market is surrounded by eager shoppers but the stall holder is delaying business bartering over the quality and price of his merchandise with a passer-by. Eventually, bored with the conversation, the time waster saunters off without making a purchase. The stall holder prepares to serve the next customer but finds that the queue has diminished because many of his customers have become tired of waiting.

Keyword PROCRASTINATION

Element Earth   *Planet* Venus

Degree 10

The maypole is freshly painted and has brightly coloured ribbons hanging from its top. Groups of children dance round the pole, weaving the ribbons into an intricate pattern. Historians recognise the symbolism and heritage of the maypole; the children merely find the dances an amusing diversion.

Keyword SIMPLICITY

Element Earth   *Planet* Venus

Degree 11

Whilst his neighbours are busy chopping wood for the winter, a popular though idle homesteader talks away the hot summer hours, leaving himself with little fuel laid up. Such is the nature of the man, lazy or not, that with the winter he tours the houses of his friends where he is made welcome and is able to share the warmth of their fires.

Keyword RESOURCE

Element Earth   *Planet* Mercury

Degree 12

In a smart and plush office a bank manager sits pensive. He has just refused a loan to a failing businessman who has dejectedly left the premises. Although the bank manager had the power to grant the loan, he did not wish to perpetuate stress and suffering by doing so. Still he cannot avoid feeling himself a traitor.

Keyword REGRET

Element Earth   *Planet* Mercury

Degree 13

The rhinoceros has the build and destructive ability of a tank. Its sheer bulk and uncertain temper has kept it safe from predators for countless millennia. Like so many other creatures it is not immune to bullets, and for nothing more important than its short fibrous horn it has been hunted to the brink of extinction. Being so large it is easy to track and kill.

Keyword DIMENSION

Element Earth   *Planet* Mercury

Degree 14

With little else to do all day but keep her house meticulously clean, the wife of a prosperous businessman takes a great pride in her home. Such is the obsessive nature of the woman that she even tidies around visitors who drop crumbs or spill cigarette ash. All too soon she has no-one but herself to appreciate the pristine abode.

Keyword TOLERANCE

Element Earth   *Planet* Mercury

Degree 15

Spending hours in preparation, bathing and adorning herself, a young woman is certain that this procedure makes her more attractive and alluring. Her friend, a bright and happy person, but one who is less meticulous about her appearance, is never short of friends and has more time to appreciate them.

Keyword MODERATION

Element Earth   *Planet* Mercury

Degree 16

An old tailor sits with needle in hand, marvelling at the quality of the cloth he is presently engaged upon. He observes and appreciates the beauty in the weave, recognising not only the mill, but the very machine that manufactured the cloth. The tailor is by no means a rich man but would gladly make up this suit for nothing if it were necessary.

Keyword APPRECIATION

Element Earth

Planet Mercury

Degree 17

Working long hard hours the farmer constantly keeps an eye on the weather, which can thwart all his efforts at a single stroke. The farmer would not change his life style despite the worries, but neither can he alter the climate.

Keyword LIMITATIONS

Element Earth

Planet Mercury

Degree 18

After weeks of practice, singers in a West End show about to open feel they have never performed more miserably. Despite their best efforts nothing is going right. When opening night arrives the performance is flawless and well received.

Keyword TREPIDATION

Element Earth

Planet Mercury

Degree 19

In any Christian church the alter with its crucifix and adorn-
ments is the focal point of worship. Though the congregation
face in this direction and are attentive to the ministrations of
the priest, most of those attending realise that God's presence
is not restricted to this one small area.

Keyword REALISATION

Element Earth   *Planet* Mercury

Degree 20

Watching only from a distance, an unsure and shy young
man admires an attractive and vivacious woman. The same
situation continues for some months until eventually the young
woman is married. It is not until years later that the admirer
learns from a third party that the object of his affection would
have welcomed his advances at the time.

Keyword NOW

Element Earth   *Planet* Mercury

Degree 21

The ruling princess of a certain kingdom is faced with the
necessity of marriage, primarily to produce an heir. The husband she chooses must be content to remain a consort all his
life and will always live in the shadow of his wife. The possible
choices for the princess are very few.

Keyword DILEMMA

Element Earth   *Planet* Saturn

Degree 22

Loud applause greets a famous actor who walks out on stage to open in a new play. So bright are the lights, he cannot see the audience, yet because of the noise he knows they are present. The actor plays his part to the disembodied sounds. Since few members of the audience know him personally the actor too is an illusion as far as they are concerned.

Keyword OBSERVATION

Element Earth   *Planet* Saturn

Degree 23

Finding himself left with a roll of cloth that has not proved to be popular, a draper considers how best to dispose of it without losing money. Eventually he cuts it into small pieces and places it amongst a box of remnants, at an apparently cheap price. Now being offered the material in a form that appears to be a bargain the roll is quite quickly sold.

Keyword INGENUITY

Element Earth   *Planet* Saturn

Degree 24

Returning from a long journey, a father brings his child an expensive present packed in a large cardboard box. After viewing the gift for some time the child spends several hours more playing with the box.

Keyword OPTIONS

Element Earth   *Planet* Saturn

Degree 25

In a remote country hamlet most villagers are pleased to welcome the van salesman who, by visiting them each week with his groceries, saves them from long and tedious trips into town. The local farms send their produce to the cities, the same merchandise with which, in one form or another, the van salesman returns.

Keyword PUZZLE

Element Earth   *Planet* Saturn

Degree 26

Popular, because of his prompt deliveries, a town milkman thrives and becomes prosperous. Having built his round personally, he finds it easy to maintain. The work is healthy and pleasant. Another milkman in the same town, working for a large combine, views his work as being laborious, cold and poorly paid, considering the effort involved.

Keyword ALTERNATIVES

Element Earth   *Planet* Saturn

Degree 27

Because of recent over exertion the feet of a ballet dancer are cut and sore, as a result of which she is advised not to dance for some time. Such is the power of the music as she waits in the wings undecided before the next performance that she carries on with her programme and feels no pain.

Keyword COMPULSION

Element Earth   *Planet* Saturn

Degree 28

The screams of delight and excitement can be heard all around the fairground as children and adults alike enjoy the thrills offered by the many rides and sideshows. The owner of the fairground sits in his plush and stylish caravan, busy with his accounts, deaf to the pleasure that, in his need to earn a living, he has created.

Keyword ABSENCE

Element Earth   *Planet* Saturn

Degree 29

The noise and clamour of a bottling plant in a dairy is a far cry from the peaceful country meadows where cows graze to produce the milk. If milk were green, perhaps those who drink it would appreciate better the sunshine and rain that feed us today, as they always have.

Keyword COMPREHENSION

Element Earth   *Planet* Saturn

Degree 30

Being successful at apprehending poachers, the gamekeeper has a reputation of efficiency. His employer is duly grateful and increases the keeper's salary. Reflecting upon this, the gamekeeper smiles to himself later as he loads an illicitly won salmon into his car. He will take it 15 miles to a town where he can sell it to a hotelier who is not choosy as to its origin.

Keyword DECEPTION

Element Earth   *Planet* Saturn

Ⅱ

GEMINI

What is this peace for which we seek?
Have we stopped to question without the incessant
need for discussions? A choice must be made between
the two, war or music. Look into the depths of
fathomless space, listen with the ear of your soul and
surely you must hear, beyond the clamour of silence
the music of the
spheres.

Degree 1

Whilst training to be a deep sea diver, a student cheats by copying the answers from a colleague's paper during an examination. Months later, whilst diving to repair an underwater installation, the individual encounters a faulty oxygen valve and in rising to the surface too quickly suffers unnecessary physical problems.

Keyword VISION

Element Air   *Planet* Mercury

Degree 2

An artist creates masterpieces of a superb quality in the style of old masters, passing them off as genuine. Such is his talent that even experienced art critics are fooled. The paintings sell well, though the artist has a studio full of his own work that nobody wishes to buy.

Keyword SELF-DECEPTION

Element Air   *Planet* Mercury

Degree 3

Two students are asked, during a lecture, to speak for five minutes each on a subject which is totally alien to their personal experience. One rambles on aimlessly for the full time allowed, whilst the other declines to talk, on the grounds that he fails to relate to the subject. The persistent gabbler receives no marks whilst the individual who said nothing is marked highly.

Keyword RECOGNITION

Element Air   *Planet* Mercury

Degree 4

During a lecture on handwriting, a graphologist is offered a specimen of script to analyse. She is busily telling the audience about the psychological problems of the individual concerned, stressing the need for concentration and effort on the part of the sample writer, when she suddenly realises that the piece of script was written by herself.

Keyword REALISATION

Element Air   *Planet* Mercury

Degree 5

In a large and populous kingdom, the monarch constantly keeps his jester in attendance for, or so the courtiers think, his amusement and diversion. When the monarch's advisers disagree or are party to treachery and intrigue, the ruler relies on the unbiased and honest advice of his fool for many of the day to day decisions that will affect millions of people.

Keyword ALTERNATIVES

Element Air   *Planet* Mercury

Degree 6

Working for a local newspaper, a journalist is intent on getting a story from a local councillor. His editor has impressed upon him the importance of the task to such an extent that although the journalist passes the scene of a bank robbery, worthy of national news coverage, he continues on his journey to the town hall.

Keyword VISIONLESS

Element Air   *Planet* Mercury

Degree 7

In a rural village, a particular young man is classified as being an imbecile. Not trusted with responsibilities he idles away his time in play and amusement. When a plague strikes the community a great percentage of the population succumbs. The imbecile does not understand the implications of the pestilence and miraculously survives.

Keyword NONCONFORMITY

Element Air   *Planet* Mercury

Degree 8

Asked to act as an intermediary in a border dispute, a diplomat is uncertain how to bridge the gap between the two sides. Despite being aware that arms and supplies are running low for both protagonists. he approaches each faction telling them how strong and powerful their opponents are. Soon a peace treaty is signed.

Keyword SUBTERFUGE

Element Air   *Planet* Mercury

Degree 9

Telling a tale in dramatic tones and deliberately embroidering the plot, the story teller speaks of a battle held many years previously. A simple and unpretentious old man sits in the crowd of attentive listeners. He is a veteran of the battle being spoken of and though he enjoys listening to the narrative he does not recognise the event to which the story teller relates.

Keyword TIME

Element Air   *Planet* Mercury

Degree 10

Supposedly one of our closest relatives in the animal kingdom the gorilla is a gentle giant. Never displaying his great strength unless forced into an unavoidable situation, even male gorillas are protective of their young. Though ranging far to find the vegetable diet they relish, gorillas will never destroy an area beyond its ability to recover.

Keyword CONSIDERATION

Element Air   *Planet* Mercury

Degree 11

For many years, thousands of satisfied patients frequented the premises of an apparently qualified physician. Known in the district as something of a miracle worker, he is one day exposed as being a fraud and a quack. Despite his past success, he is no longer visited by his patients.

Keyword BELIEF

Element Air   *Planet* Venus

Degree 12

For many years a shoplifter is successful in evading detection, such is her ability as a thief. Eventually, despite her best endeavours, she is seen and apprehended. Appearing in court she admits only to the particular offence that she has been charged with, despite the fact that the very clothes she is wearing were stolen from the same store at an earlier date.

Keyword EVASION

Element Air   *Planet* Venus

Degree 13

On first impression one could be forgiven for believing that a talented parrot must have the highest intelligence rating amongst birds. He does not merely speak individual words but is capable of reciting whole passages. Alas, speech without comprehension does not represent intelligence, for the parrot merely mimics and has no understanding of what he says.

Keyword DECEIT

Element Air   *Planet* Venus

Degree 14

Two men must undertake the same journey on a hazardous road to deliver messages. One of the individuals, because of his superior persuasive ability, manages to convince the other that there is little point in them both risking a dangerous undertaking and is able to convince his less quick witted friend to take his message for him.

Keyword PERSUASION

Element Air   *Planet* Venus

Degree 15

Ants appear to be individual entities for they each have bodies and movement unique to themselves. A closer study however reveals that each ant is only an extension of the whole colony, for any reasoning ability and planning is possessed only by the ant colony as a whole. The ants nest could therefore be considered to be one life form.

Keyword CO-OPERATION

Element Air   *Planet* Venus

Degree 16

An errand boy must make several trips in the same district, but has to keep returning to the shop to reload his bicycle. After a little thought he loads all of the merchandise at once onto a handcart and although the journey is longer than one trip would take on the bicycle, overall he saves a great deal of effort and time.

Keyword INSPIRATION

Element Air   *Planet* Venus

Degree 17

Reading a historical diary is a person whose knowledge of the calendar is limited. He notices entries for the 23rd and 25th October of a particular year and therefore assumes that during the year in question the month of October did not contain a 24th day. When he explains this to a friend he cannot understand the humorous reaction he receives.

Keyword OBSERVATION

Element Air   *Planet* Venus

Degree 18

Too high and exposed for plants to be able to withstand the severity of the climate, a mountain peak appears stark and barren. A closer inspection of the rocky outcrop reveals nooks and crannies where nesting birds find protection and shelter. The lack of foliage close by is no detriment to the birds who can fly elsewhere to feed.

Keyword APPEARANCES

Element Air   *Planet* Venus

Degree 19

The doorway of a building is neither outside nor inside, but can be considered to be both. When the door is shut and you are outside, you cannot perceive what is within. Conversely, if you are inside the building with the door shut, you cannot experience what is without. Only when you stand between the two can you be aware of both realities.

Keyword DUALITIES

Element Air   *Planet* Venus

Degree 20

Approaching his employer, a worker asks for a raise in his salary. The employer explains in detail the financial constraints governing the lack of money available. The employee mulls over the problem on the way home on the bus, which is passed at the first set of traffic lights by the employer in his large and expensive luxury saloon car.

Keyword RELATEDNESS

Element Air   *Planet* Venus

Degree 21

Arriving at the house of a rich merchant, a messenger is tired after the long journey. The master of the house insists that the messenger rests and eats before delivering his news. During the intervening period the merchant, who is elderly, is suddenly taken ill and dies. The messenger cannot now deliver the words he was charged with so that the news, good or bad, is irrelevant.

Keyword CONSIDERATION

Element Air   *Planet* Uranus

Degree 22

At a holiday centre, a ventriloquist's skill has a tremendous effect on a child who has visited the centre during the summer. Years later the child, now a young adult, once again meets the ventriloquist. Memories of the artiste have faded but he immediately recognises the puppets when he is shown them.

Keyword SELECTIVE

Element Air   *Planet* Uranus

Degree 23

To save space in his farmyard and fields a farmer builds his hay ricks larger than the size which has been the pattern for generations , and in close proximity to each other. When one of the ricks bursts into flames, due to spontaneous combustion, all the hay is destroyed in minutes.

Keyword CONFORMITY

Element Air   *Planet* Uranus

Degree 24

Travelling the country and rarely stopping for more than a week in one place, an able and hard working craftsman is regularly offered permanent employment but always refuses. He does so because his work and friendship, he believes, will never be a source of irritation to others if all see him as new, interesting and a source of curiosity.

Keyword DIVERSITY

Element Air   *Planet* Uranus

Degree 25

In the heavy, smoke-laden atmosphere of a plush hotel restaurant, members of an exclusive club sit captivated by the verbal dexterity, wit and impeccable diction of a great orator. Meeting the speaker later, club members are surprised to be confronted by a shy, retiring individual with a pronounced stammer.

Keyword CIRCUMSTANCE

Element Air

Planet Uranus

Degree 26

With a deft flick of the wrist, the conjuror produces a live dove from beneath a silk square. All the members of the audience are well aware of the deception they have been subjected to, but nevertheless they watch eagerly. One onlooker is disappointed however because he knows how the trick is performed.

Keyword PERSPECTIVE

Element Air

Planet Uranus

Degree 27

Born within minutes of each other, a pair of identical twins are separated shortly after birth. One rises high in life, whilst the other occupies a more lowly position. Despite their differing fortunes, their looks and basic characteristics remain absolutely identical until the day of their death.

Keyword INEVITABILITY

Element Air

Planet Uranus

Degree 28

During a war, a town is besieged but has plenty of supplies and could last a considerable period. A rumour starts that infiltrators have been planted in the community. The suspicion of hostility thus created weakens the collective strength of the town so much that the inhabitants become less disciplined and the attackers are able to gain entry.

Keyword SUSPICION

Element Air   *Planet* Uranus

Degree 29

Greyhounds on a racing track do not necessarily appreciate that they are competing. For them the objective is to catch the automatic hare that always stays in front of them. Time after time they fail to catch the hare and yet on each occasion they still endeavour to do so.

Keyword TENACITY

Element Air   *Planet* Uranus

Degree 30

Because of differing atmospheric pressures, the needle of a barometer can point in varioust directions. This indicates the most likely weather. In the eyes of those who look at the device it would appear that the mechanism has some skill to actually predict the future. The painted face of the barometer hides the mechanism behind.

Keyword OBSERVATION

Element Air   *Planet* Uranus

ZODIAC SIGN 4

CANCER

*Can the Sun stand even for a moment
in heaven when movement is irrepressible?
So it appears. Look again and search
diligently with the no-mind that encompasses complete
knowing. All that is perceived is the farthest extent of
the pendulum's swing, where all physical
laws cease to have accustomed validity.
Here is the everlasting
now.*

Degree 1

The amount of information that a baby absorbs immediately after birth is colossal. Few people would guess to look at such an apparently helpless, innocent and feeble creature, the incredible sifting, sorting and correlation of knowledge and information that is taking place.

Keyword HIDDEN

Element Water   *Planet* Moon

Degree 2

Because of the length of time he has been in the trade, and the skill he has amassed, the baker does not need to weigh the ingredients he mixes for batches of bread each day. His new assistant, after a short while, tries to copy his employer's example with disastrous results. The bread is too salty and does not rise sufficiently.

Keyword EXPERIENCE

Element Water   *Planet* Moon

Degree 3

After some months employed in a busy public house, a pretty and friendly barmaid has learned not to take too seriously the teasing she receives from some of the regulars. The strange fact is that when she meets the same individuals in the street, they are often shy in her company.

Keyword ALTERNATIVES

Element Water   *Planet* Moon

Degree 4

Tossed by stormy seas in mid Atlantic many weeks from home, a round-the-world yachtswoman considers her reasons for undertaking such an arduous solo task. She is wet, miserable and cold, and cannot at present quite understand her own motivation. It was clear enough when she embarked and will be so again once the journey is over.

Keyword HESITANCE

Element Water   *Planet* Moon

Degree 5

A small brook that meanders and slowly follows a centuries chosen path, is destined eventually to become the raging torrent that, now a river, surges on impatiently to the sea. The brook is the river and also the sea. For though the name and the force differs, the water involved is the same.

Keyword TRANSFORMATION

Element Water   *Planet* Moon

Degree 6

Safe inside its protective adopted shell, the hermit crab's only basic vulnerability lies in its inability to remain the same size. Periodically it has to find a larger shell and must, for a short time at least, leave itself open to attack, bereft of its protective armour.

Keyword VULNERABLE

Element Water   *Planet* Moon

Degree 7

Left to burn in a still and quiet room the flame of a candle does not waver or fluctuate. Should the smallest of draughts be allowed to pervade the calm air of the room, the candle flame bends against the current of air, consuming the wax unevenly and spilling it unburned.

Keyword FLUCTUATION

Element Water   *Planet* Moon

Degree 8

Having performed its mating ritual, a drake no longer takes any interest in the rearing of its family. The duck herself patiently builds a nest, lays the eggs and sits on them, not to mention taking care of the chicks once they have hatched. For all his selfish behaviour, the process still could not take place without the drake's contribution.

Keyword NECESSITY

Element Water   *Planet* Moon

Degree 9

For many centuries it was a total mystery where eels disappeared to when they undertook their long journey down to the sea. Like many migratory aquatic species, despite their long journey, possibly as far as the Sargasso Sea, they can still find their way back to the very stream where they themselves were spawned.

Keyword INSTINCT

Element Water   *Planet* Moon

Degree 10

Gathered together only once each year, a certain family can feel secure, even if only temporarily, in their collective identity. Individual members of the family rarely have any contact at all throughout most of the year but on this one evening their individual lives are of little significance.

Keyword COHESION

Element Water   *Planet* Moon

Degree 11

After long hours of patience waiting on the river bank a fisherman decides to take some lunch. Moving away from the rod no more than a few feet, he sees the float dip for the first time all day. Before he can get back to the rod his bait has been taken and the fish has escaped.

Keyword ATTENTIVENESS

Element Water   *Planet* Mars

Degree 12

A homeworker becomes bored with the day to day routines that have become her lot and decides to embark on a part time post in a local factory. Very soon the sheer monotony of the process she is placed upon, which simply necessitates pressing a button, helps her to appreciate the variety that her housework could sometimes present.

Keyword REALISATION

Element Water   *Planet* Mars

Degree 13

The elderly caretaker takes his usual evening stroll around the deserted building. Although the property has been condemned and is due to be demolished in a matter of days, the caretaker still replaces spent light bulbs and carefully sweeps the corridors. It is his intention that the building should be spotless when the demolition team arrives to destroy his world for good.

Keyword DILIGENCE

Element Water   *Planet* Mars

Degree 14

For many years the beam streaming forth from a lighthouse protecting a rocky outcrop has prevented countless ships from coming to grief. One night the mechanism becomes faulty and takes several hours to repair. The night in question has a full moon and consequently no ships run onto the rocks for they can see the silhouette of the lighthouse.

Keyword TRUST

Element Water   *Planet* Mars

Degree 15

Since mankind first lifted its head to gaze at the evening sky the Moon has been the object of the closest scrutiny and reverence. Despite the fact that the Moon shines in reflected glory, courtesy of the Sun, its significance to the Earth and to man has always been individual and unique.

Keyword SELFSUFFICIENCY

Element Water   *Planet* Mars

Degree 16

On many occasions, despite her skill and training. a midwife does very little when presiding at the birth of a baby that any other reasonably competent individual could not achieve. Her presence offers confidence against the contingency that problems may just possibly arise.

Keyword PRECAUTION

Element Water   *Planet* Mars

Degree 17

A new recruit into the Merchant Navy is warned by all his shipmates of the rigours of sea sickness which they assure him strike all new mariners. The recruit is surprised that he does not experience such problems, despite a rolling and pitching ocean on the first night at sea. Later he has need to see the First Officer but is turned away because the man is suffering from sea sickness.

Keyword PARADOX

Element Water   *Planet* Mars

Degree 18

Facing a potentially difficult problem politically, the Queen of a particular Kingdom, whose husband is too ill to make decisions, decides to preside in his absence. Those in attendance believe the instructions that they are given to be from the King himself. Thanks to the deception, enemies of the State never discover the potential vulnerability caused by the King's illness and so cannot utilise the situation.

Keyword DECEPTION

Element Water   *Planet* Mars

Degree 19

Washing day sees members of a community boiling gallons of water. It takes many hours to do so and would be laborious and hard work save for the companionship and co-operative efforts of the people involved. Their congenial banter and willingness to support each other makes an unpleasant task into a socially meaningful event.

Keyword RELIANCE

Element Water   *Planet* Mars

Degree 20

Alone for most of the night with no company, a solitary night-watchman spends hours staring into the glow of his brazier, reliving events in his past. The pictures in the coals are a comfort to him and make a lonely night pass quickly.

Keyword VISION

Element Water   *Planet* Mars

Degree 21

A delivery boy is stopped by the police when on his early evening rounds and accused of having no rear light on his bicycle. A closer inspection reveals that the bulb is shining as brightly as ever but that the reflective backing is rusty and dull.

Keyword DISCOVERY

Element Water   *Planet* Neptune

Degree 22

Like clear glass in any ordinary house the richly ornamented stained glass of churches serves the primary function of letting light into the building. Both sorts of window provide for the same basic requirement but it could not be suggested that the comparison ends with this simplest of functions.

Keyword OPTIONS

Element Water   *Planet* Neptune

Degree 23

Having arived at the same port many times, the Captain of a cargo ship has never totally understood the necessity of having a harbour pilot aboard to steer what seems to be a quite straightforward course. One dark and turbulent night he is grateful for the pilot's expert knowledge and realises that circumstances can throw up many variables.

Keyword CONFIRMATION

Element Water   *Planet* Neptune

Degree 24

Looking at a tree from a distance a casual observer has no comprehension of the many processes taking place behind the bark. He cannot observe the sap rising or falling, neither can he view the growing processes which take place continually.

Keyword PERSPECTIVE

Element Water   *Planet* Neptune

Degree 25

On a busy seafront a shrimp seller does brisk business with holiday makers who are anxious to try the fresh caught produce of the local ocean. The shrimp seller does not inform the public with whom he deals that the merchandise he sells was caught days ago and on the other side of the world.

Keyword ASSUMPTION

Element Water   *Planet* Neptune

Degree 26

Graceful and majestic, a willow bends in apparent supplication, bowing its regal branches towards the life giving water that has allowed it to gain strength, whilst at the same time preserving its supple nature.

Keyword RECOGNITION

Element Water   *Planet* Neptune

Degree 27

A sheep dog at work displays a type of controlled natural behaviour. It appears to follow the shepherd's instructions to the letter in rounding up and returning sheep to him. In the wild it would use the same procedure to head prey towards the rest of the pack whilst hunting.

Keyword UTILISATION

Element Water   *Planet* Neptune

Degree 28

Because a mother fails to be consistent in the way she treats her child, he is confused and fails to respond to any discipline, never really knowing what is expected of him. When in the company of more consistent adults the child is comfortable and well behaved.

Keyword CONFORMITY

Element Water   *Planet* Neptune

Degree 29

In the depths of a tangled and thick jungle an explorer happens upon a hitherto unknown tribe of great composure and natural beauty. After spending some enjoyable days in their company the explorer deliberately loses the map reference to their whereabouts.

Keyword PRESERVATION

Element Water   *Planet* Neptune

Degree 30

A very rich and slightly eccentric person rents a market stall in the local town and spends the day not selling a commodity but trying to give away new bank notes to the shoppers. When he takes stock at the end of the day he is disappointed to see that only two or three people have suspended their preconceptions of life enough to accept his genuine and generous offer.

Keyword BELIEF

Element Water   *Planet* Neptune

♌

L EO

A power is thrown down
and the vanquisher becomes the vanquished.
Humility drinks freely at the well of heroism,
unaware and unconcerned about an account of the
battle that few know to be falsehood.
The water is pure, sweet and
satisfying.

Degree 1

The animator is aware that his individual pictures, when filmed in order and replayed, will appear to be moving in an ordered sequence. Through the medium, events impossible for actors to perform can be created, an illusion can become a reality.

Keyword ILLUSION

Element Fire   *Planet* Sun

Degree 2

Boasting of his success on the track, the racing driver now on the road in a private car becomes so busy talking that he fails to negotiate a bend in the road and runs the vehicle into a ditch.

Keyword CONCENTRATION

Element Fire   *Planet* Sun

Degree 3

Waiting in the yard of a busy factory the owner of the establishment views his pocket watch and admonishes those workers who do not arrive on time. At the end of the day he does not thank those workers who work a few extra minutes, concerned to finish properly the tasks they are involved in.

Keyword FAIRNESS

Element Fire   *Planet* Sun

Degree 4

Throughout history the circle has been used to portray perpetual existence. It is the very essence of unchanging certainty and the promise of universal eternity. In mathematics however the circle is worth absolutely - nothing!

Keyword TRANSCENDENT

Element Fire   *Planet* Sun

Degree 5

Gifted, or alternatively cursed, with an over sensitive conscience, a child who has argued with her parents tries to make amends by willingly running errands and endeavouring to be generally useful. The forgiveness in the parents is their willingness to allow the child to behave in this way.

Keyword ACCEPTANCE

Element Fire   *Planet* Sun

Degree 6

An individual walking along a narrow beam placed upon the ground experiences no fear of falling from the beam and so accomplishes the task easily. If the length of wood were placed high in the air, only extensive training could blot out the consequence of a mistake.

Keyword PERSPECTIVE

Element Fire   *Planet* Sun

Degree 7

Two workers are overlooked by the same foreman. Because they have different personalities, he encourages one but often reprimands the other. Each worker knows a different foreman, yet they both view the same man.

Keyword REALITY

Element Fire   *Planet* Sun

Degree 8

Because he has the power of life and death over his subjects a King is viewed by them as being all powerful. The monarch himself is possessed of a scolding wife and the wife's greatest fear is the power inherent in the people if they should choose to unite and rise.

Keyword PROBABILITY

Element Fire   *Planet* Sun

Degree 9

Many people accuse a rich philanthropist of being false because they believe that the good he does for the poor is merely a means of feeding his own ego and also a way of justifying his riches, yet without his generosity many people may have starved.

Keyword MOTIVE

Element Fire   *Planet* Sun

Degree 10

Having lost all senior officers in a battle, a hitherto quiet and ineffectual junior officer assumes command of a group of soldiers. Immediately the officer proves to be a competent leader at a time of great difficulty.

Keyword OPPORTUNITY

Element Fire   *Planet* Sun

Degree 11

A lavish state banquet is held to entertain foreign emissaries who have arrived to try and negotiate a peace treaty between two antagonistic factions. Although the country holding the feast is poor and can ill afford the expense the treaty is negotiated and the ensuing peace allows economic growth to improve the country's financial standing.

Keyword EVENTUALITY

Element Fire   *Planet* Jupiter

Degree 12

Despite warnings from all sides about the certainty of a difficult economic situation ahead, a businessman optimistically keeps ploughing money into his factory. When the minor slump is over he is able to expand the business quickly because he did not run down his capacity or work force.

Keyword CONFIDENCE

Element Fire   *Planet* Jupiter

Degree 13

Though not entirely without merit because of the magnificent spectacle it represents, the display of a peacock is of little evolutionary importance unless there are females in the vicinity. The entire procedure is an elaborate mating ritual.

Keyword FLAMBOYANCE

Element Fire   *Planet* Jupiter

Degree 14

Despite its power and co-operative hunting ability, the lion is essentially a lazy animal. Unless hungry, it spends most of its time lying in the sun or idling away the hours in play. It will even steal the catch of some other predator given the opportunity.

Keyword LETHARGY

Element Fire   *Planet* Jupiter

Degree 15

Universally speaking, our Sun is not particularly large, yet without it neither the Earth nor any living creature upon it could exist. We are totally dependant on this star and yet only a minute fraction of the Sun's power reaches the Earth. Most is lost to the endless depths of icy space.

Keyword DEPENDENCE

Element Fire   *Planet* Jupiter

Degree 16

An ageing theatre is condemned to be demolished and the situation is the cause of angry protests by local residents who remember the theatre's former glory. The building has been closed for many years but only when the intention to knock it down becomes clear do the protests start.

Keyword REALISATION

Element Fire   *Planet* Jupiter

Degree 17

Bystanders watch with interest the filming of a scene destined for a popular television series. The fact that the watchers see stage directions and hear the participants talking and behaving as their true life selves does not undermine their belief in the characters as they will ultimately appear in the finished programme.

Keyword IMAGINATION

Element Fire   *Planet* Jupiter

Degree 18

On the platform at a political meeting, a politician reads his pre-written speech. In dramatic tones he deplores the conduct of the present government of his country, extolling the virtue of the party he is certain will soon be brought to power. He has heard and read the same speech so many times before that he has actually begun to believe that one day things will genuinely be different.

Keyword DELUSION

Element Fire   *Planet* Jupiter

Degree 19

Arriving in her home port after a protracted period abroad, where she has been successful financially, a young woman is pleased with her efforts and has been longing for her homeland for a long time. In a very short time she realises that in her absence, either she or her country has changed and so she sets off on her journeys again.

Keyword EXPECTATION

Element Fire   *Planet* Jupiter

Degree 20

Having spent all his life teaching a particular branch of philosophy to his students, a well known teacher suddenly changes his entire point of view. He is aware that he cannot unteach his former students but is equally certain that his revised viewpoint is the correct one.

Keyword REVISION

Element Fire   *Planet* Jupiter

Degree 21

For many months a bounty hunter has tracked a wanted criminal and has at last cornered him in a small town. The transgressor has built himself a peaceful and law abiding life, having repented his past follies. The bounty hunter sees only the money involved and insists on returning the criminal for trial.

Keyword KARMA

Element Fire   *Planet* Mars

Degree 22

Having joined a religious sect that fundamentally disagrees with her early learning, a teenager finds she has become the cause of bitterness within her family. Though they agree that her moral code and basic beliefs are sound, they cannot accept her personal need to follow a different path.

Keyword TUNNEL-VISION

Element Fire   *Planet* Mars

Degree 23

There are many metals more valuable in terms of their potential uses than gold and yet throughout countless ages men have been willing to steal, cheat and even kill on its account. Like any other metal it is only precious in relation to man's need to possess it.

Keyword AVARICE

Element Fire   *Planet* Mars

Degree 24

Trying to show his genuine affection in the only way open to him, a millionaire spends vast amounts on trying to secure the love of his daughter. He is heartbroken when she slopes off with a penniless nobody and cannot understand the difference between the love he showed his daughter and the love she ran away to find.

Keyword MISUNDERSTANDING

Element Fire   *Planet* Mars

Degree 25

A visitor to a foreign country finds himself in trouble with the law over certain remarks he has made regarding the government. His intention was not to cause trouble, he was merely joking. He failed to recognise that the culture was very different from his own and that under certain circumstances a joke can appear to be an insult.

Keyword FORETHOUGHT

Element Fire   *Planet* Mars

Degree 26

Having for many years charged nothing for his services, a healer is at last forced by economic necessity to demand a fee. Though he is certain that people may think twice about consulting him, he is surprised to discover that his clientele doubles in a matter of days.

Keyword NEED

Element Fire   *Planet* Mars

Degree 27

Utilising a toy gun a robber holds up a bank and demands that a bag be filled with money. The teller turns away to fill the bag and later when the thief has chance to check his haul he discovers that he has been given nothing but useless pieces of blank paper.

Keyword JUSTICE

Element Fire   *Planet* Mars

Degree 28

A general who has been successful in many campaigns and much decorated by his nation, takes part in a military coup to overthrow what he considers to be a repressive government. Unfortunately he is a better soldier than he is a politician and within weeks is himself displaced and totally discredited.

Keyword SPECIALISATION

Element Fire   *Planet* Mars

Degree 29

Whilst performing all season for only the pleasure of the competition, a gifted young athlete does extremely well. Representing her country at the Olympics however her nerve fails. In a subsequent event she forgets the circumstances of the competition and starts to enjoy herself. In the process she wins a medal.

Keyword PROPORTIONS

Element Fire   *Planet* Mars

Degree 30

Domestic cats, even if well fed, rarely lose the ability or desire to hunt. Birds or rodents often fall prey to this efficient and merciless predator. The advantage of retaining the hunting skill could mean the difference between life and death if at any time a particular animal were forced to fend for itself.

Keyword NECESSITY

Element Fire   *Planet* Mars

♍

VIRGO

*The world turns from season to season,
what was once sterile is now bearing fruit. Out of
nothing comes forth all the bounty that nature can
bestow. Apart and separate the word and the principle
grow in unison, following a determined path and never
being diverted by the mind of man. The pattern may
not be swayed but it can be understood.
Through understanding comes knowledge,
from knowledge springs the
solution.*

Degree 1

Working long into the night, an accountant checks and re-checks row after row of figures that he is certain contains an error which, despite his avid scrutiny, he cannot find. Eventually he conceded temporary defeat and goes home. Next day, fresh and alert, he discovers the mistake in minutes.

Keyword FATIGUE

Element Earth   *Planet* Mercury

Degree 2

A great breakthrough is announced concerning treatment of a terrible disease, the effects of which have incapacitated tens of thousands of people. To the eyes of the public the discovery of the new drug seems like instant success, though to the people concerned, it represents years of painstaking research.

Keyword PERSISTENCE

Element Earth   *Planet* Mercury

Degree 3

Viewed on paper, the Architect's plan for a new high rise development appears to be a superb answer to housing shortages. His plans fail to show the social isolation, filth, graffiti and vandalism that will mar the objectives of his concept.

Keyword IMPLICATION

Element Earth   *Planet* Mercury

Degree 4

Alone in his office the Astrologer carefully checks his calculations and realises that his client is due for a fairly difficult period to come and that he must now decide how specific to be in his consultation. Ten minutes prior to the consultation the Astrologer finally makes up his mind and tears up the offending chart. His conscience pricks but fortunately the client fails to meet the appointment.

Keyword ALTERNATIVE

Element Earth   *Planet* Mercury

Degree 5

After months of effort a hard working author puts the finishing touches to a long and complex novel. Since the book is more or less assured of general success, the writer could take a long break before commencing a subsequent work, but through the last couple of chapters of his present book new ideas have started to emerge which force him to commence immediately.

Keyword IMMEDIACY

Element Earth   *Planet* Mercury

Degree 6

In a Temple situated in the Western World stands a Buddah that was a present from an old and revered establishment in the Far East. The statue shows a happy rotund figure, serene and all wise. Although the cultural differences between East and West are so obvious, the Buddah himself still smiles in the busy industrial city.

Keyword TRUTH

Element Earth   *Planet* Mercury

Degree 7

Intent on the book she is reading, a child is also walking to the shops, performing an errand for her parents. Because of the nature of the story, the child, even whilst walking, is absorbed by the tale and lacking concentration is knocked down by a car. Although only shaken the child has learned a valuable lesson about apparent realities.

Keyword CONCENTRATION

Element Earth   *Planet* Mercury

Degree 8

Deep in the virtually inpenetrable jungle an ordered and well planned garden grows behind a high wall. In the midst of the garden is a maze of great complexity. The jungle makes the garden almost impossible to find and the maze is difficult to traverse. In the centre of the maze is a locked box. The box is empty.

Keyword QUEST

Element Earth   *Planet* Mercury

Degree 9

In terms of status within a Victorian household, a Governess found herself to be a social outcast. She was not one of the family nor was she considered to be one of the servants and was usually forced to spend most of her time in the company of children. On her day off each week she did at least have the option to travel away from her place of employment to a local town, there to enjoy the same anonymity as all the other people she encountered.

Keyword POSITION

Element Earth   *Planet* Mercury

Degree 10

Because of the cultural as well as the language problems, a young interpreter is having a difficult time trying to assist two high powered emissaries at an international conference. She is aware that she could cause offence by a misinterpretation but at the same time must ensure that she does not over embellish or otherwise alter the fundamental meaning of phrases from either side.

Keyword ATTENTION

Element Earth   *Planet* Mercury

Degree 11

During his rounds a postman has been depressed by the number of bills and circulars that he has been obliged to deliver, and senses that as a result his arrival has not always been welcomed. Without thinking, he passes a house where he hardly ever calls, the lonely occupant of which would be pleased with a communication of any kind.

Keyword COMMUNICATE

Element Earth   *Planet* Saturn

Degree 12

A merchant on business in a distant and strange land is allowed to take a look in the treasure store of a rich and ancient temple. As he scans the wealth of gold and silver that he beholds, he makes a mental assessment of the value of some of the items. Such a valuation would never be possible in the eyes of the monk who shows him round, for he sees only spiritual worth in the collection.

Keyword VALUES

Element Earth   *Planet* Saturn

Degree 13

Divided from his neighbours by a high fence a householder feels secure within his own house and garden. One day a high wind demolishes the fence and for the first time the householder talks in depth with his neighbour. So much does he enjoy the conversation, the next fence he builds is considerably smaller.

Keyword KNOWLEDGE

Element Earth   *Planet* Saturn

Degree 14

Owing to pressure of work, a printer delays starting to print a medical book that has just been released. His present labour is nothing more important than a frivolous and unsavoury magazine and while he works upon it, people who could gain real benefit from the new treatments in the medical volume continue to suffer.

Keyword PROCRASTINATION

Element Earth   *Planet* Saturn

Degree 15

Having read thousands of manuscripts in her career, a literary agent one day passes up a book which, if she did but know it, is destined to become a colossal best seller. This is the first manuscript ever sent to her that she has failed to scrutinise properly. She ensures that such a mistake is never repeated.

Keyword DISTRACTION

Element Earth   *Planet* Saturn

Degree 16

A certain business executive is given to underestimating the value of his secretary. Despite the tremendous assistance she represents to him, he is often offhand and rude to her. When he is on holiday, business continues as usual but when she is away the work piles up awaiting her return.

Keyword BLINDNESS

Element Earth   *Planet* Saturn

Degree 17

During a crucial tennis match and with the game all but even, one of the players becomes extremely temperamental and vehemently questions the call of "Out" from a line judge. Even though in his heart he knows the call was good, the tennis player goes on arguing until he totally upsets his own equilibrium and subsequently loses the game.

Keyword SELF DEFEAT

Element Earth   *Planet* Saturn

Degree 18

For years a philosopher spends his time in trying to assess the essential truths and correct the failings within humanity. Never having worked outside the educational environment which he has always known and rarely mixing socially with people below his own intellect, the philosopher in question fails dismally to understand why all his efforts are doomed to failure.

Keyword PERCEPTION

Element Earth   *Planet* Saturn

Degree 19

Because of early disciplines and having always been subject to a rigid moral code, a young woman has chosen to remain a virgin until the day prior to her marriage. Her new husband, who has not been so abstemious, has never the less respected her point of view during their relationship. He is surprised when on the night before the wedding his prospective bride breaks her self-imposed vow with only a few hours left before the ceremony.

Keyword CHOICE

Element Earth   *Planet* Saturn

Degree 20

With an over large case load and little or no assistance, a social worker toils many hours beyond her expected working week and, despite her tiredness, genuinely tries to help her clients. To each of the people she assists there are no other clients and they see the social worker as belonging just to them.

Keyword VISION

Element Earth   *Planet* Saturn

Degree 21

Suspended high above the ground, the parachutist, when first having left the aircraft, appears to change his sense of reality very little. It is only when he drops nearer the ground that the surroundings telescope on his vision and the landing site, which when viewed from the aircraft was only a small part of a whole, now becomes the most important reality.

Keyword ALTERATION

Element Earth   *Planet* Venus

Degree 22

Bees have a sophisticated and efficient means of communication. Constant touching of antennae, one insect to another, can pass sensory messages extremely quickly. The hive could not exist without information regarding food supply, its location and relevant geographical information.

Keyword INTEGRATION

Element Earth   *Planet* Venus

Degree 23

Being one of the strongest of the English Tudor monarchs, Queen Elizabeth I was considered by most of her subjects and by the Church to be, in a religious sense, on favourable terms with the Almighty. When important decisions had to be made, this fact did not prevent her from consulting an astrologer, who together with all such luminaries was frowned upon by the church.

Keyword CONTINGENCY

Element Earth   *Planet* Venus

Degree 24

Inside and outside Europe, Paris is regarded with a reverence granted specifically to this one City. Its treasures and sights, together with its history, place it as being one of the artistic and cultural gems of the world. Despite this fact, it has brothels, run down housing and social problems in abundance.

Keyword HIDDEN

Element Earth   *Planet* Venus

Degree 25

The wild boar, during the middle ages, was considered to be one of the most prized animals, both for its flesh and the sport it offered. Capturing the creature was no easy task. Armed with vicious tusks and possessing a mean and fiery disposition, a boar is well able to kill a man with one charge.

Keyword DEFENCE

Element Earth   *Planet* Venus

Degree 26

Down a quiet country road a cyclist slowly pedals, drinking in the picturesque surroundings. He covers little distance compared to a motorist who is able to achieve his destination much faster. The motorist however has to concentrate so hard that he has little time to appreciate nature's beauty, nor can he smell or hear the subtle signposts that mark his route as the cyclist does.

Keyword OBSERVE

Element Earth   *Planet* Venus

Degree 27

A person can talk incessantly for the sake of the sound he or she makes, but this is no sign that the speaker says anything that is worth knowing. On the other hand, a casual remark can carry tremendous significance sometimes.

Keyword SPONTANEITY

Element Earth   *Planet* Venus

Degree 28

The silence of the library is shattered by a young librarian who accidentally drops a large pile of books. Embarrassed she stoops to pick them up, noticing with a wry smile that the last book is entitled, 'How to make an instant impression on others.'

Keyword COINCIDENCE

Element Earth   *Planet* Venus

Degree 29

Lying for days in a coma, a girl injured in a motor accident eventually regains consciousness. She cannot remember the accident or the ensuing period and although consciously they never happened for her, she is assured by the nursing staff that the period involved has elapsed. The fact that she accepts the situation is due to her logic and can never be substantiated by her personal awareness.

Keyword TIME

Element Earth   *Planet* Venus

Degree 30

A young man builds model aircraft and is discovered one day by a friend, working on the tiny model pilot from one of his aircraft. The pilot is less than two inches tall. The modeller, holding a magnifying glass and a super fine paintbrush, is asked what he is labouring at so intently. It turns out that he is painting medal ribbons on the pilot's jacket, though the figure will barely be discernible when fitted into the cockpit.

Keyword PRECISION

Element Earth   *Planet* Venus

LIBRA

*The heart and the feather upon the balance
are etched in stone, frozen in time and safe in the
darkness for millennia. Locked into the sediment since
the world began what is their reality more than
in the mind? The same feather could balance
the whole earth until the end
of time.*

Degree 1

A spring balance needs no counter-weight. The object being weighed is balanced by a spring housed within the machine itself. The accuracy of the device depends entirely upon the design and manufacture of its components, for if it registers the wrong weight on the scale, the machine is of no use whatsoever.

Keyword INVENTIVE

Element Air   *Planet* Venus

Degree 2

Trying to capture the essential 3-dimensional characteristics of an athlete, a sculptor tries again and again to perfect the clay model. Eventually the artist changes slightly the stance of the model who poses for her and discovers that the new pose is less difficult to translate to the medium.

Keyword FINENESS

Element Air   *Planet* Venus

Degree 3

Feeling genuine compassion for urchins who sleep rough in the street, a Victorian philanthropist sets up an orphanage for such children. Though now fed and clothed, in their patron's absence the children are subject to a harsh form of discipline and humiliation that they never had to encounter whilst living rough.

Keyword ALTERNATIVE

Element Air   *Planet* Venus

Degree 4

Prior to a concert, a pianist composes himself and practises finger exercises in his dressing room. Every performance is as unnerving as the first and each one takes a great toll on his nervous system. Only when the concert is over does the maestro realise, in some small measure, what his gifts are.

Keyword COMPREHEND

Element Air   *Planet* Venus

Degree 5

Long after the reality of a romantic and happy evening has passed, a young woman, who on that first night encountered the joy of love, remembers the warmth of a caress and the heady perfume of the evening air. The romance may not last, but the memories will.

Keyword RECALL

Element Air   *Planet* Venus

Degree 6

The rut is over and soon the proud stags will lose their antlers. What were, during that brief period, wild, aggressive and dangerous animals, now revert to becoming merely a component part of the herd. They can be observed grazing pensively with the rest of their kind.

Keyword INTERLUDE

Element Air   *Planet* Venus

Degree 7

Man has often sensed the intelligence inherent in his aquatic cousin, the dolphin. The language to communicate with these bright creatures may never be discovered. Perhaps this is because, despite our similarities in some ways, we simply have nothing to say to each other.

Keyword SEPARATE

Element Air   *Planet* Venus

Degree 8

Well aware that on the evening, his act is not being well received, a comedian continues with his usual routine, despite the fact that the audience is restive and even insulting. On the previous night however, the same jokes had brought the house down.

Keyword FLEXIBLE

Element Air   *Planet* Venus

Degree 9

Because of his artistic interests and general appearance, a particular young man is often thought of as being effeminate. Of course, most people recognise his right to be whatever he wishes, though one or two people do ridicule and taunt him. Eventually, tired of the harassment, the man moves away from the district but finds that wherever he travels the ignorant few continue to be intolerant.

Keyword ESCAPE

Element Air   *Planet* Venus

Degree 10

Customers marvel at the colourful display of blooms in the florist's window, which brighten up a cold and cheerless winter's day. Many of the flowers are artificial but even these can be appreciated against the snow and sleet of January.

Keyword REFUGE

Element Air   *Planet* Venus

Degree 11

Being unpopular with many of her associates, a woman is accused of being flirtatious to the point of trying to steal her friends' partners. Because it is her basic nature to behave the way she does, the woman finds it hard to change, or even understand why, on the one hand she gets on so well with men, but cannot seem to make friends within her own gender.

Keyword SEARCH

Element Air   *Planet* Uranus

Degree 12

Spending much time at Court, a young Duke has the reputation of not only being gallant but also charming. He is elected as the Queen's champion and henceforth defends her honour in all his actions. His own wife leads a miserable life in the country, with few diversions and little or nothing to occupy her mind.

Keyword UNDERSTANDING

Element Air   *Planet* Uranus

Degree 13

In the confines of a small hotel, during the out of season period, it is obvious that a young couple who have recently arrived are on their honeymoon. It is the couple themselves who telegraph the fact, so obviously do they endeavour to hide it. Were they to act as if they had just married, perhaps nobody would have noticed.

Keyword DISGUISE

Element Air   *Planet* Uranus

Degree 14

If you were left an ornament to take care of by a friend whilst he or she were away for a protracted period, would you hide the object in a cupboard, fearing for its safety in case burglars called, or would you put it on display to enhance your home and remind you of the friend who will eventually return?

Keyword UTILISE

Element Air   *Planet* Uranus

Degree 15

Three astronauts look down from their orbiting spacecraft to the Earth far below. Though they are all aware of the differences in their respective lives previously and, as a result of this experience, they will all change greatly, though in radically different ways. Never the less they all look towards the Earth with the same love.

Keyword COMMUNION

Element Air   *Planet* Uranus

Degree 16

Despite the noise and clatter of an unruly class, a young and inexperienced school teacher does her best to get on with the lesson in hand. She knows that one child near the back of the class is showing interest and in the mind of the teacher the rest of the class ceases to exist. To the child too, the surrounding commotion is blotted out by her interest and her desire to learn.

Keyword MICROCOSM

Element Air   *Planet* Uranus

Degree 17

It has always been considered a necessary prerequisite of a certain carnival that the maiden, taking part as the Queen of the ceremony, should be pure in every sense of the word. Because of the delicacy of the situation, after a while the question is no longer asked directly. As a result and to be reasonably certain, a younger girl is chosen with each passing year.

Keyword TRUTH

Element Air   *Planet* Uranus

Degree 18

After his performance, resting back stage, an opera singer condescends to see two fans who have been waiting patiently outside for some time. The event is of little consequence to the international star, for he sees admirers almost every day, but is a once-in-a-lifetime occasion to the adoring fans themselves.

Keyword PERSPECTIVE

Element Air   *Planet* Uranus

Degree 19

A party is in full swing when a neighbour arrives to try and quieten the event down, for he has been trying to sleep. Although he arrives in an angry frame of mind he is soon pacified by the party-goers and despite his intention to go straight back to bed, he is one of the last people to leave the house.

Keyword PARTICIPATE

Element Air   *Planet* Uranus

Degree 20

Children out on a picnic do not appear to notice the flies and other insects which gather to help enjoy the feast taking place, nor are they bothered by the occasional chill breeze that might upset adults present. Perhaps children are too busy enjoying themselves to pay attention to such trivialities.

Keyword CONCENTRATION

Element Air   *Planet* Uranus

Degree 21

The swan is a beautiful creature. Its grace of form and regal bearing set it apart from other birds. Under the saintly and pristine exterior however, the story is very different. Swans are birds of volatile and aggressive temperament and have wings powerful enough to break a human arm.

Keyword APPEARANCE

Element Air   *Planet* Mercury

Degree 22

Laying in bed night after night, a child is terrified by the wardrobe which stands at the end of the bed. On the eve of her birthday, the child's mother puts her presents in the wardrobe. Once she has conquered her fear enough to retrieve the presents, the child henceforth views the wardrobe with far less trepidation.

Keyword DOUBT

Element Air   *Planet* Mercury

Degree 23

A fussy and awkward customer accuses a greengrocer of possessing scales that are set in his favour. When he proves conclusively that any aberration in the scales accuracy is clearly in favour of the customer she is satisfied. However, she does not offer to pay for all the extra vegetables she has had at the greengrocer's expense for a number of years.

Keyword BALANCE

Element Air   *Planet* Mercury

Degree 24

A Judge, about to pass sentence on a criminal, is aware, prior to the judgement, of the laughter of children who are playing outside in the street. The offender before him is not long out of childhood and the Judge decides to give him another chance. He passes a suspended sentence.

Keyword COMPASSION

Element Air   *Planet* Mercury

Degree 25

Working all day with gold and precious stones, the jeweller designs and creates delicate and fashionable settings. His expertise is not in doubt but the craftsman could never afford to buy for himself any of the jewellery he creates.

Keyword IRONY

Element Air   *Planet* Mercury

Degree 26

The windmill owes its efficiency not only to the great vanes that drive the grinding stones but also to the small vane or paddle at the back of the mill that keeps the windmill facing into the prevailing wind. Without this device the mill could only work on certain days.

Keyword UNDERTONE

Element Air   *Planet* Mercury

Degree 27

Many great ships were once built and repaired in the now deserted dockyard. Most of the vessels are now only a memory, having been scrapped years before. Although the yard itself has not been in use for years, so solidly was it built that it might well outlive the next generation of ships also.

Keyword CONTINUITY

Element Air   *Planet* Mercury

Degree 28

Broken barrels in a brewery all find their way to the cooper, whose art goes back many hundreds of years. The tools he uses have not changed significantly in all that time, nor have the techniques involved. The skill lies not in the methods but in the precision which, like his ancestors, the cooper gained only by experience.

Keyword LEARNING

Element Air   *Planet* Mercury

Degree 29

In the final of an important competition a golfer mislays his favourite putter. He blames losing the contest on the absence of the club in question, though the one he borrowed was of identical manufacture and weight.

Keyword KNOWLEDGE

Element Air   *Planet* Mercury

Degree 30

An aged music hall entertainer who was once a household name is now rarely recognised in the street. For a brief period, songs and routines from his era come back into fashion and for a short while the entertainer is once again in demand. After the interlude he is cast back into his accustomed obscurity.

Keyword PERIODICAL

Element Air   *Planet* Mercury

♏

SCORPIO

Darkest of dark, deepest of deep.
The end marks a moment to begin and the very
darkness appears as a cloak to mask the magician's
deception. True magic is cloaked in light,
known to all, yet truly understood only by the
enlightened, perpetually
ignorant.

Degree 1

The surgeon's hands are both his skill and his living, so he is dejected when they are damaged in an accident. As his bitterness passes, he finds himself teaching others his skills, and acquires a verbal dexterity to do so that he never possessed before. Even when his hands eventually heal, he does not go back to his former existence.

Keyword CIRCUMSTANCE

Element Water   *Planet* Mars

Degree 2

As anyone who touches a nettle, or worse still falls into a bed of them, knows only too well to their cost, the sting of the plant can be both irritating and painful. The gardener who dons leather gloves however, grasps and uproots the plants with immunity.

Keyword PROTECTION

Element Water   *Planet* Mars

Degree 3

In the closing stages of a marathon, a particular runner is forcing himself on with determination alone. Mile after weary mile he urges and pushes his exhausted body forward. After the race he spends many days recovering mentally and physically from the self imposed ordeal but considers the suffering to have been worthwhile. His finishing position was twenty-fourth.

Keyword TENACITY

Element Water   *Planet* Mars

Degree 4

Alone and quiet in a padded cell, a woman branded as a lunatic because of a single mistake made early in life, considers her situation. Her recent violent outburst only confirms the opinion of her doctors that she is unstable, though the woman herself sees her actions as quite rational in view of the frustration she is forced to endure.

Keyword OPINION

Element Water   *Planet* Mars

Degree 5

A lumberjack holds the record for the number of trees felled in a single month. He and his colleagues are well aware of the animosity felt towards them by conservationists who feel that the trees should be preserved. For the last twenty years, in his spare time, the lumberjack has been creating elegant and beautiful reproduction furniture.

Keyword MULTI-FACETED

Element Water   *Planet* Mars

Degree 6

Being a master of his craft, the scissor grinder daily pushes his cart round the streets of a busy city and is always welcomed by the housewives who value his skill. The scissor and knife sharpener is aware of his usefulness but does not return too quickly to the same district for he knows that a partly sharp knife will not cut through frugality as surely as a dull one.

Keyword PERCEPTION

Element Water   *Planet* Mars

Degree 7

An engineer designs and builds a steam locomotive more efficient and streamlined than any previously built. He is proud of his achievement as it rolls out of the station for the first time. Two hours later the locomotive is wrecked as a result of a faulty track, that, in his love affair with his creation, the engineer has failed to have replaced.

Keyword OVER-VIEW

Element Water   *Planet* Mars

Degree 8

Almost everyone is apprehensive about the dentist, though in actual fact the majority of such practitioners are gentle and rarely cause any discomfort to their patients. The greatest fear however, is generated within those people who have not taken care of their teeth adequately and therefore spend the longest period sat in the dentist's chair.

Keyword PREVENTION

Element Water   *Planet* Mars

Degree 9

Calculated risks are part of the stuntman's life. Every day he dives through windows or leaps from balconies. When asked by friends, who admire his skill and athletic ability, if he will accompany them on a rock climbing expedition, the stuntman declines, declaring the pastime to be too dangerous.

Keyword LIMITATION

Element Water   *Planet* Mars

Degree 10

Devastating all before it, a plague sweeps through Western Europe. A certain small village is affected and though the inhabitants know they could escape into the surrounding countryside, they are also aware that they may carry the infection with them. Unanimously they decide to close their village to the outside world until the plague has run its course amongst them.

Keyword UNDERSTANDING

Element Water   *Planet* Mars

Degree 11

In the back streets of a large city, an experienced, though now elderly, barber carries on his trade. Because his technique is neither stylish or modern, young people tend to avoid his premises. One day, while passing a larger and more fashionable hair stylist in a more up-market part of town, he discovers from pictures in the window that the styles he has maintained for years are now back in fashion, but at ten times the price.

Keyword FULL-CIRCLE

Element Water   *Planet* Neptune

Degree 12

Deserted after a week long event, except for a few local children, a huge arena stands quiet. The children are playing at racing on the running track and are ragged urchins from a shanty town close by. One of the older children, unseen by cheering crowds and with no stop watch to monitor him, breaks several world records on the track.

Keyword REALITY?

Element Water   *Planet* Neptune

Degree 13

Mightiest of the big cats, the tiger is a supreme hunter. Efficient and deadly, she stalks through the tangled jungle or over rolling plains. Yet for all her ferocity in the kill, and despite the tremendous power in her feet and claws, back in the lair with her cubs she is a responsive and gentle mother.

Keyword VARIABLE

Element Water   *Planet* Neptune

Degree 14

Having little choice after arriving late at a battle site, a commander chooses the less favourable bottom of the hill, having noticed the fallen snow and anticipating a rising wind. His opponent is jubilant and orders his archers to advance down the hill. Soon the wind blows snow into their faces and because they cannot see, their arrows fall short. At the bottom of the hill, the opposing archers pick up the fallen arrows and fire them back, with the wind. In this way the battle is won.

Keyword UTILISATION

Element Water   *Planet* Neptune

Degree 15

In folklore and legend, snakes have always been partly revered and partly hated. Often representing the Devil in western culture, where it is not particularly prevalent, the snake has, in countries with a greater number of species, attracted a rather more regal status. Unknowing, the snake continues to slither about as it has done for hundreds of thousands of years.

Keyword PERSPECTIVE

Element Water   *Planet* Neptune

Degree 16

Busy and a little flustered, a tired nurse stops to adjust the pillow of a patient. The person in the bed looks at the tired face and smiles. As the nurse surveys the trusting, grateful invalid, her exhaustion passes away and she continues her duties with a lightened step. Her compassion is her cure.

Keyword HEALING

Element Water   *Planet* Neptune

Degree 17

An excess of garlic in the diet is likely to lead, in western society at least, to a certain amount of social isolation, for the smell of the plant is pungent in the sweat or on the breath of those that consume it. Never the less, garlic cleans the stomach, purifies the blood and is virtually undetectable to the individual that has eaten it too.

Keyword ALTERNATE

Element Water   *Planet* Neptune

Degree 18

At the scene of a road accident, a passerby takes charge of the situation, dressing the wounds of the injured and saving the life of one. When the emergency services arrive, the hero slips away quietly, unwilling to be recognised as a former doctor who was dismissed for unprofessional conduct years before.

Keyword PRESENT

Element Water   *Planet* Neptune

Degree 19

A vixen out hunting steals from flock containing two lambs, one of which is sickly. The shepherd gives chase and eventually the vixen drops the lamb. By the time the shepherd returns to the flock, he discovers that the vixen has doubled back in his absence and taken the healthy lamb.

Keyword THOUGHT

Element Water   *Planet* Neptune

Degree 20

The vineyard does not require particularly good soil. Vines will grow in the most difficult of places, provided they have sufficient heat and water. Growing where other crops might well fail, this remarkable plant is turned, with the help of humanity, into liquid sunshine.

Keyword RESILIENCE

Element Water   *Planet* Neptune

Degree 21

For years a certain business executive has maintained an extremely hectic and stressful career, and is proud of his company's success. Eventually, through overwork, he falls ill for a lengthy period and is astonished to discover that the company survives without him.

Keyword IMPORTANCE?

Element Water   *Planet* Moon

Degree 22

Strange and apparently horrific devices are laid out neatly in the sterile operating theatre. Though at first glance having the appearance of an ultra clean torture chamber, the room offers new life to many who are brought within its confines.

Keyword APPEARANCE

Element Water   *Planet* Moon

Degree 23

Unobtrusive and retiring, the scorpion is a lover of dark corners and will rarely show itself. Silent to the world at large, the creature enjoys a hermit like existence. However, should it be disturbed or cornered the creature has a vicious sting and courage to tackle adversaries many times its own size.

Keyword CAUTION

Element Water   *Planet* Moon

Degree 24

One night a policewoman with little strength or experience, is confronted whilst alone by a serious street fight. Although very much afraid, she commands the combatants to stop fighting. Such is their surprise at the sight of the diminutive lady and her manner with them, that the protagonists cease brawling immediately and disperse in an orderly manner.

Keyword COMMAND

Element Water   *Planet* Moon

Degree 25

Elegant and proud is the old cockerel, who from his first herald of dawn, struts about, protecting the hens and guarding his domain. In this, his habitat, the cockerel is king, but like all the fowl in the run, he could all too easily fall prey to a fox if he is not vigilant.

Keyword CAUTION

Element Water   *Planet* Moon

Degree 26

A veteran soldier spends his days relating tales of former glories to any passerby who is willing to listen. In his own town his stories are well known and generally disbelieved. Upon his death, amongst his possessions are found a number of medals. These, for the sake of modesty, the veteran never wore. Amongst them is a Victoria Cross.

Keyword BELIEF

Element Water   *Planet* Moon

Degree 27

Aided by his ugly looks and the generally unsavoury nature of his life-style, the vulture must rank highly amongst the most hated of birds. Disliked or not, the animal is an essential part of the food chain, for in dealing quickly with carrion, the vulture helps to eliminate disease and filth.

Keyword NECESSITY

Element Water   *Planet* Moon

Degree 28

Any person who wanders too close to a tannery when the wind is in the wrong direction will certainly find the smell vile and offensive. If the same person were to walk into a saddlery or leather shop, they would probably remark upon the distinctive and pleasant smell of new cured leather.

Keyword CIRCUMSTANCE

Element Water   *Planet* Moon

Degree 29

A locksmith is recruited to open a safe for which all traces of the combination have been lost. In a short time he gains entry to the safe. Noticing that inside the safe there is a considerable sum of money, he charges a larger fee than would normally be customary. The client for whom he has been working pays the fee and then enquires, genuinely, why the locksmith has never used his skills criminally?

Keyword WORTH

Element Water   *Planet* Moon

Degree 30

An unsightly scrapyard is visited by a pompous council official who asks the proprietor why he has not filled in certain documents which were sent to him. The scrap dealer explains that he cannot read or write. The official notices with some surprise the large and expensive motor vehicle outside, which obviously belongs to the illiterate scrap dealer.

Keyword ESTIMATION

Element Water   *Planet* Moon

SAGITTARIUS

*Where does the man end and the animal begin,
at what point is the liquid made solid? Draw an
arrow of adventure, string a bow of enquiry and aim
for the target of the moment. You cannot
fail to find dead centre.*

Degree 1

Whilst resident in the embassy a country's Ambassador is considered, for all normal purposes, to be living on his own country's soil. This diplomatic immunity also extends to the vehicle he travels in. In fact, despite the fact that he is an alien in a foreign land, he is often more privileged than the citizens of the state in which he is resident.

Keyword ANOMALY

Element Fire   *Planet* Jupiter

Degree 2

Feigning affluence, a young salesman in need of orders, spends his last few pounds on entertaining a potential client. He ensures that he is observed tipping liberally and generally sparing no expense. His ploy works and he secures a sizable order, despite the fact that the client has seen through his pretence.

Keyword TRUST

Element Fire   *Planet* Jupiter

Degree 3

The Emperor of a powerful state is in a quandary concerning a decision of national importance. His two main advisors disagree about a solution. In the end, the Emperor takes the advice of the assistant who presses home his point in the most impartial and off hand manner, for the ruler considers that the cooler the individual, the more likely will be the wisdom.

Keyword DETACHED

Element Fire   *Planet* Jupiter

Degree 4

A titled lady attends a tea party, held in the summer on the lawn of a large stately home. Although she discoursed with rich and influential people for most of the afternoon, the conversation she enjoys the most is with a maid whom she herself had employed some years previously.

Keyword APPEARANCE

Element Fire   *Planet* Jupiter

Degree 5

Participating in a contest, an archer has one arrow left with which he can either clinch or lose the prize. His coach knows that the participant will not have kept the score for himself and decides not to inform him of the importance of this last arrow. Cool, unconcerned and detached, the archer's aim is true.

Keyword UNCONCERNED

Element Fire   *Planet* Jupiter

Degree 6

Decked in finery and proud of his new status, a recently ordained Bishop prepares to officiate at his first important ceremony. He wishes to make a favourable impression but the minute before he is due to depart a helper informs him that the service has been cancelled, the reason being a small but serious fire which has broken out in the Cathedral. The Bishop is not superstitious but on a subsequent occasion he is less meticulous about his appearance.

Keyword PROVIDENCE

Element Fire   *Planet* Jupiter

Degree 7

Involved in a long and complicated court case, a Barrister, who is representing the accused, finds himself becoming more personally involved in the case than he considers to be prudent. At a crucial stage he resigns the brief, believing this to be preferable to spoiling the defendant's chances through lack of objectivity.

Keyword CONCERN

Element Fire   *Planet* Jupiter

Degree 8

An error in a column of figures is responsible for a misunderstanding of a particular company's financial situation. Trust is lost in the factory, which subsequently fails. During the winding up process the mistake is discovered but alas too late, for confidence in the company cannot be re-established at this late stage.

Keyword APPEARANCE

Element Fire   *Planet* Jupiter

Degree 9

Faced with a hypochondriac patient who feels that she is seriously ill, the physician finds it impossible to convince the patient that she is really quite well. In the end, the frustrated doctor prescribes a totally useless course of tablets and the patient leaves the surgery happy and already feeling better.

Keyword BELIEF

Element Fire   *Planet* Jupiter

Degree 10

The proud and majestic elephant can be trained, like many animals, to assist man in his work. The great beasts often perform their tasks with children sat astride their necks, encouraging the elephants by tickling them behind the ears. No amount of shouting or cruelty could achieve what these little children can.

Keyword INNOCENCE

Element Fire   *Planet* Jupiter

Degree 11

In a particular city a powerful financier is approached to back a new scientific discovery that could prove to be of tremendous benefit to mankind as a whole, but could also adversely affect many companies already trading in the same field. With an eye to the status quo, the financier refuses his assistance.

Keyword MAINTAIN?

Element Fire   *Planet* Mars

Degree 12

With honours even and everything dependant on the 18th hole, a professional golfer prepares to tee off for the last time in the match. Carefully he takes his stance but as he swings, a bird flies across his line of vision, causing him to slice the drive. Though he loses the match he does not mention the occurrence later at the presentation.

Keyword PROVIDENCE

Element Fire   *Planet* Mars

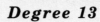

Degree 13

An illegal gaming house flourishes in a run down and seedy property in the red light district of a city. Those who play the tables are aware of the chances they take and though they know that a police raid could take place at any time, the possibility only heightens the excitement of their gambling.

Keyword CHANCE

Element Fire   *Planet* Mars

Degree 14

Whilst hunting deer in a forest clearing, an experienced marksman sees a stag that he recognises. On many occasions in the past he has tried to shoot the stag, but each time the wily animal caught wind of him at the last moment and fled. The animal is now old and stately but the hunter chooses to leave it and search for other sport.

Keyword COMPASSION

Element Fire   *Planet* Mars

Degree 15

Spending a fair percentage of her working day on the telephone, a woman whose task is to sell insurance, repeats on each occasion the usual patter but rarely obtains a favourable response. Through insults and rebukes she remains impassive, ignorant of all but the occasional positive reaction she achieves.

Keyword CONCENTRATION

Element Fire   *Planet* Mars

Degree 16

The young ward of an elderly and seemingly disinterested businessman is surprised to find himself in the position of inheriting the old man's fortune in its entirety. The ward, never expecting a penny, always treated his benefactor without ceremony or reverence, a fact that others, not mentioned in the will, might have been prudent to emulate.

Keyword NATURAL

Element Fire   *Planet* Mars

Degree 17

After a weary and hard fought case in a high court, a prisoner has been found guilty as charged. The weather during the proceedings has been very hot and everyone in the stuffy courtroom is warm and exhausted. The Judge calls for a lengthy adjournment before passing sentence, in order to cool off and review the case carefully and rationally.

Keyword WAIT

Element Fire   *Planet* Mars

Degree 18

Prior to the start of a race and mounted on his favourite horse, a jockey, who has performed well during the season, waits for the starting gates to open. The time sat in the starting stall, though only seconds, as always, appears to be much longer than the duration of the race.

Keyword RELATIVE

Element Fire   *Planet* Mars

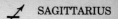

Degree 19

A millionaire asks for the bill, having eaten in a plush and exclusive restaurant. Calling the head waiter across the customer quibbles over a minor error in the charge, which amounts to a few pence. The waiter immediately rectifies the bill in the customer's favour, assuming that the millionaire is likely to be correct. How else would he have achieved his present financial position?

Keyword BELIEF?

Element Fire   *Planet* Mars

Degree 20

Reviewing the work of two artists, a critic despises the work of one painter, who has many canvases on display, whilst praising the efforts of another, who has only one small sketch available for the exhibition. The criticism is not entirely limited to artistic quality or style but is partly affected by the critic's eye to the future for he too is also a dealer.

Keyword PERCEPTION

Element Fire   *Planet* Mars

Degree 21

With a host of successful seasons behind him, a footballer of international reputation retires from playing whilst still at the pinnacle of his career and immediately embarks upon a career in management. The player considers that a manager straight from success will inspire the same in others and he knows work will not be hard to find.

Keyword SHREWDNESS

Element Fire   *Planet* Sun

Degree 22

Dusting and polishing in a large house, a maid carelessly knocks over a valuable piece of porcelain, it falls to the floor and shatters into a dozen fragments. She informs her employer of the accident but instead of being annoyed, the owner of the house pays the maid the value of the broken item. Now consciously more careful, the maid never breaks another item.

Keyword VALUATION

Element Fire   *Planet* Sun

Degree 23

Wandering along the paths and amidst the quiet glades of a huge garden, a privileged visitor, allowed to meander thus, in what to the public at large is a private domain, feels at ease in this environment. The owner of the garden has money, the visitor has none, but then the owner of the garden is so busy making money to run the house and keep the garden, that he has no chance to stroll pensively.

Keyword RESPITE

Element Fire   *Planet* Sun

Degree 24

A professional darts player in the final of an international competition, requires only double top to win the championship. Poised to throw the dart, the competitor remembers the first game he ever played as a child and of the thrill of realising his natural talent for the sport. His concentration lapses monetarily and yet his aim is true.

Keyword LESSONS

Element Fire   *Planet* Sun

Degree 25

Certain inlets and ports on the Continent of Antarctica are becoming blocked, because of a build up of algae. This difficult to remove and productive life form in earlier times caused no problems because it was the main source of food to thousands of whales, which man has seen fit to hunt to the brink of extinction.

Keyword CONSEQUENCE

Element Fire   *Planet* Sun

Degree 26

The political prisoner is freed from detention by a new political regime, though he is still advised not to express his radical opinions in the press. The dissident leaves his native land for he realises that he is just as much in prison in his own home as in the confines of the jail.

Keyword CONFINEMENT

Element Fire   *Planet* Sun

Degree 27

Jupiter is the largest of the planets in our solar system, though much of its huge surface is covered by poisonous gas. It is named after the King of the Gods, proving that though we may still have scientific doubts about its effect upon the Earth, the ancients had confidence in their own judgement, based on generations of observation.

Keyword SCALE

Element Fire   *Planet* Sun

Degree 28

A social worker has doubts about her reasons for the work she has undertaken on behalf of her clients and feels that it may have been undertaken to feed her own ego. Thousands of grateful individuals who have benefited from her advice and assistance could not care less about what has motivated her efforts.

Keyword SELF-CRITICISM

Element Fire   *Planet* Sun

Degree 29

With the Budget imminent, the Chancellor of the Exchequer has to please, if such were possible, all elements of society and yet still make the books balance. He may choose to hit one section of the community very hard instead of spreading the burden across the whole cross section of society.

Keyword BIAS

Element Fire   *Planet* Sun

Degree 30

Having been in possession of a legacy, a young man has been extravagant in his lifestyle and squandered the money at his disposal. Though he does not regret having spent the money in the way he did, he is still aware that he could have used it to better ends.

Keyword OBSERVATION

Element Fire   *Planet* Sun

♑

CAPRICORN

Rage and struggle all you will,
for no matter how great the torment, the bonds that
secure you will hold fast. Think the rope unwoven,
consider the hemp not grown. Make the seed wither
back into the mists of no time that ever was.
Where is the Scape Goat now.
Behold, you are free.

Degree 1

Standing upon the most elevated part of his property a farmer gazes down at the vista below. From the hill he can observe, in a single sweeping glance, all the sheep and cattle contentedly grazing on the lush green pasture. The farmer feels that from this height he could hold the whole farm in the palm of his hand. The effort expended in looking after the farm appears ridiculous when viewed from this vantage point.

Keyword PERSPECTIVE

Element Earth   *Planet* Saturn

Degree 2

With work scarce, a bricklayer is obliged to assist in the construction of a rather shoddy housing estate. The bricklayer is annoyed at having to build sub-standard houses, all the more so because he knows that one day work will be plentiful but these miserable dwellings will still exist.

Keyword CARE

Element Earth   *Planet* Saturn

Degree 3

Consider a recently bankrupted individual, who is suddenly in possession of a brilliant idea to make money. He cannot raise sufficient funds to commence his project because of his bankruptcy, but he could sell the plan to someone who does have sufficient money but few ideas.

Keyword OPTION

Element Earth   *Planet* Saturn

Degree 4

Because of the peace and quiet of his surroundings the man wielding the spade is very happy. The healthy outdoor life, free from the restrictions and tedious routines of his contemporaries, make this individual the epitome of contentment. Reflecting upon his luck he turns back to continue digging the grave that he has recently commenced.

Keyword VIEW

Element Earth   *Planet* Saturn

Degree 5

Even the families of miners would have difficulty telling their menfolk apart at the end of a shift, so black are their faces. Only when they emerge from the bath house do the miners once again appear to be the recognisable individuals that they really were all the time.

Keyword DISGUISE

Element Earth   *Planet* Saturn

Degree 6

A trapped pot holer has spent hours in the cold and damp of a cramped, dripping cave, prior to rescuers reaching him. Despite the ordeal, a few weeks later he is once again exploring the twists and turns of the same musty cavern.

Keyword EXPERIENCE

Element Earth   *Planet* Saturn

Degree 7

How can we believe in the passing of time as it is displayed by the hands of a clock? When we are employed in an enjoyable pastime the clock's hands virtually fly round, whilst if one is undertaking a tedious chore, the same hands hardly appear to move at all. All the same, both tasks will be over eventually.

Keyword REALITY

Element Earth   *Planet* Saturn

Degree 8

An elderly lady is observed to have become apparently bored by social contacts and disinterested in company. A routine medical examination by chance discovers that she has developed a hearing defect. The hearing aid, with which she is fitted, restores her interest in the conversation around her.

Keyword AWARENESS

Element Earth   *Planet* Saturn

Degree 9

Many men have been labouring for days, digging in terrain where normal machinery cannot be used. After some time a specialised excavator is delivered and manages in a few short hours, to remove more earth than the men have been able to do in a week or more.

Keyword SPECIALISATION

Element Earth   *Planet* Saturn

Degree 10

Who is the better man? The miser, who through pettiness and meanness, spends a lifetime building up a huge fortune, or his only relative, a cheerful but none too careful man, who squanders the entire fortune within weeks of the miser's demise.

Keyword CLASSIFY

Element Earth   *Planet* Saturn

Degree 11

Goats are adaptable enough to survive on just about any sort of food. In the wild they prefer mountainous regions and are invariably timid when faced by man. Their greatest capacity is their ability to utilise the most unlikely foothold in their quest for the summit.

Keyword ADAPTABILITY

Element Earth   *Planet* Venus

Degree 12

A trainee complains that the brick hod he is obliged to carry is too heavy for him to move around quickly and asks for a smaller receptacle. His employer refuses, knowing that the hardest way at first can condition the individual more quickly in the long run.

Keyword PERSISTENT

Element Earth   *Planet* Venus

Degree 13

Feeling his house to be too cold and his heating bills too large, a householder purchases a wood burning stove. So busy is he, henceforth, finding and chopping wood, that he barely has time to feel the benefit of the fire. The exercise helps to keep him warm as well as fit.

Keyword INGENUITY

Element Earth   *Planet* Venus

Degree 14

A husband is convinced that his wife is involved in a clandestine love affair and as a result makes her life a constant misery with his checking on her movements and accusations of her infidelity. After several years, his irrational behaviour drives her to the very practice he has always thought her to be guilty of.

Keyword OWNERSHIP

Element Earth   *Planet* Venus

Degree 15

If a length of rope breaks and is repaired by a correctly tied knot, it is a fact that the rope becomes stronger at the knot than anywhere else on its length, despite this having been the site of the rope's failure.

Keyword REPAIR

Element Earth   *Planet* Venus

Degree 16

Having been employed for general fetching and carrying duties a labourer constantly advises his employer about effort saving devices that would make the job simpler. Eventually the employer dismisses his employee, buys the devices and does the fetching and carrying himself.

Keyword MINDFULNESS

Element Earth   *Planet* Venus

Degree 17

As a paid soldier, a mercenary is not obliged to believe in the cause for which he fights. To him killing is a lucrative job of work and nothing more. However, a soldier from the opposing faction who receives a bullet wound would not stop to question the moral convictions of the firer.

Keyword CONVICTION

Element Earth   *Planet* Venus

Degree 18

Medieval stone masons employed on a magnificent edifice such as Canterbury Cathedral must have known that they would live and die, never seeing the completed building upon which they laboured. It is possible that their satisfaction was achieved in small sections, skilfully completed, which would one day be appreciated as a part of the whole.

Keyword CONCEPTION

Element Earth   *Planet* Venus

Degree 19

Believing a somewhat dilapidated terrace of houses to be an eyesore, a local council clears the site and builds high rise flats. The new tenements are expensive and generally unpopular, losing money for the council. Meanwhile, terraces such as the one that has been destroyed become fashionable and worthy of renovation.

Keyword CONSIDERATION

Element Earth   *Planet* Venus

Degree 20

Sitting on the corner of a busy street a beggar rattles the small tin which he holds in his hand at passersby. Some individuals put pennies in the tin, others ignore the beggar. A few even cross the street to avoid him, not realising that he cannot admonish their meanness with a scowl since he is blind.

Keyword RESPONSIBLE

Element Earth   *Planet* Venus

Degree 21

Within his lonely cell a prisoner plots his escape in detail, the plans being the result of months of painstaking consideration. At last, within two days of his possible parole, the prisoner puts his plan into action but is quickly apprehended. With no chance now of parole, the prisoner starts planning again.

Keyword OPPORTUNIST

Element Earth   *Planet* Mercury

Degree 22

A stranger visiting a wheelwright's shop might have difficulty in understanding the hotch potch of different parts that combine to create one cart wheel. No matter how well all the pieces fit, and no matter how accurately they are made, only the rim, created by a blacksmith and not the wheelwright, will hold the final pieces together.

Keyword CO-OPERATION

Element Earth   *Planet* Mercury

Degree 23

The park attendant spends many hours in the autumn, sweeping up the leaves that nature spills all over the lawns and the paths. If leaving his task before removing the piles of leaves, such a man on his return should not be surprised to discover that the wind had undone all his good work.

Keyword COMPLETION

Element Earth   *Planet* Mercury

Degree 24

A parish priest, bored with generally accepted topics for his sermons, instead commences to tell his parishioners about his favourite pastime, which is gardening. He is surprised to find that the following week his dwindling flock has swollen to twice the usual size.

Keyword UNORTHODOX

Element Earth   *Planet* Mercury

Degree 25

The Prime Minister of a country approaches his nation's economic difficulties with pessimism and worry. Eventually he succumbs to the pressures and is forced to retire. His replacement is a naturally cheerful individual whose attitude does much to foster a greater feeling of hope in the country as a whole.

Keyword ATTITUDE

Element Earth   *Planet* Mercury

Degree 26

Travellers call to visit a hermit living in a draughty cave by the side of a road. Despite his pitiful poverty, the visitors are somewhat surprised to find the hermit to be a cheerful man. Concerning his isolation, the hermit is convinced that rare spontaneous contact with others is more meaningful than a constant babble.

Keyword MEANINGFUL

Element Earth   *Planet* Mercury

Degree 27

Hold an acorn in your hand. This diminutive seed may be destined to give rise to a mighty oak tree which could, with the passing of time, become a huge forest. Each tree in the forest would be directly traceable to that first acorn. Do you not hold a forest in your hand?

Keyword CREDIBLE

Element Earth   *Planet* Mercury

Degree 28

Having been born of peasant stock and living all her life in humble serfdom, a hard working woman is, by the changing law of her land, granted her freedom from virtual slavery. Horrified, she immediately rushes to the lord of the manor in which she lives to enquire what crime she has committed to deserve such a punishment.

Keyword DELIVERANCE?

Element Earth   *Planet* Mercury

Degree 29

A group of tourists stand and observe a tragedy being re-enacted in an ancient Greek theatre. The visitors are not familiar with the language or even the culture that inspires the performance. Despite the intentions of the original author, the exaggerated gestures and unusual costumes of the actors eventually cause the onlookers to dissolve into fits of laughter.

Keyword UNDERSTANDING

Element Earth   *Planet* Mercury

Degree 30

Ignoring the rise of technology affecting his neighbours, a farmer insists on ploughing his fields using a team of shire horses. The farmer does not act from sentiment alone. He knows his horses do not damage the good earth in his fields and he is aware also that one day the oil for machinery will be exhausted.

Keyword MOTIVE

Element Earth   *Planet* Mercury

AQUARIUS

The new age dawns
as the Earth precesses back into the future.
The maiden sees her tired reflection mirrored in pools
of water spilled from the vessels she carries. The load
is heavy and the world believes this water to be
precious. Perhaps we should realise that we
stand at the edge of a vast and
bottomless lake.

Degree 1

A captain adventurer has been weeks at sea, driven by gales and with no idea of the geographical position of his ship. Knowing full well that he and his crew will soon be in desperate need of fresh water, the captain nevertheless appears cheerful and confident. On the day the water casks run dry, land is sighted.

Keyword CONFIDENCE

Element Air   *Planet* Uranus

Degree 2

Faced with having to repair a car of foreign and unfamiliar manufacture, a motor mechanic experiences difficulty in working on the vehicle. The basic principles of the machinery are the same as any other car but the badges on the bonnet and the boot are unknown.

Keyword APPREHENSION

Element Air   *Planet* Uranus

Degree 3

An antique dealer comes across a piece of furniture that he is sure is a genuine and therefore valuable piece of craftsmanship. Despite his certainty regarding the authenticity of the article, the dealer is loath to make a purchase as the price is only a fraction of what he would expect to pay.

Keyword HESITANCE

Element Air   *Planet* Uranus

Degree 4

The responsibility for the safety of possibly hundreds of people is always uppermost in the minds of aircraft pilots. Such individuals are invariably methodical and totally committed when on the flight deck but may well be untidy and unpredictable away from the controls.

Keyword SITUATION

Element Air   *Planet* Uranus

Degree 5

Intent upon the destruction of a section of society which he sees as being corrupt, a terrorist plants a bomb in a building he knows is due to be used for a government meeting. True, the meeting will be interrupted, but many of those injured and killed will be the very 'ordinary' people the terrorist purports to support.

Keyword CONFUSION

Element Air   *Planet* Uranus

Degree 6

Many clairvoyants have accurately predicted major world events but very few such gifted people spend much of their time considering such matters. The majority would rather assist individuals in their day to day lives and thereby shun notoriety.

Keyword ROUTINES

Element Air   *Planet* Uranus

Degree 7

A group of smallholders in the same locality are each committed to making their own purchases as regards their immediate agricultural needs. The time and money thus wasted is considerably reduced once the neighbours form a co-operative and buy their requisites in bulk.

Keyword CO-OPERATION

Element Air   *Planet* Uranus

Degree 8

A commoner is present at a function frequented otherwise by peers of the realm. The fact that he carries no title leads the commoner to be rebuked by his fellow diners. He does not object in the least for in this gathering he is unique, an original.

Keyword SELF-AWARENESS

Element Air   *Planet* Uranus

Degree 9

Devastating all before it, a cyclone weaves its path of destruction across fertile farmland. In its wake, people whose lives have been shattered in seconds endeavour to pick up the pieces and salvage what little they can. The rich feel the effect of the devastating wind more than the poor, for they have more to loose.

Keyword DEGREE

Element Air   *Planet* Uranus

Degree 10

At the end of a lengthy and painful divorce case, the couple involved go for the first time, in the eyes of the world at least, their own separate ways. The marriage is now totally dissolved but it does not stop the similarity in mannerisms evolved over years between the couple while the marriage remained intact.

Keyword HABIT

Element Air

Planet Uranus

Degree 11

Busily connecting up dozens of wires according to their colour code, an electrician who has performed a similar task so many times previously finds little difficulty. Any passerby might be puzzled by a procedure that appears similar to sorting spaghetti but then they would lack the electrician's experience.

Keyword LEARN

Element Air

Planet Mercury

Degree 12

A national leader who considers himself a pacifist finds himself in the difficult situation of having to lead his country into an unavoidable war. Despite his beliefs, he does not resign since he is aware that he is at least partly responsible for the deteriorating situation.

Keyword RESPONSIBILITY

Element Air

Planet Mercury

Degree 13

Should a child who learns in his late teens that he was born illegitimately consider his life to be ruined because of the discovery? Rather, if he must look back at all, should he not reflect upon the care and concern that has been heaped upon him as he was growing?

Keyword NOW

Element Air   *Planet* Mercury

Degree 14

A junior officer is court martialled for instigating a mutiny amongst his men and is punished accordingly. Justice may be seen to be done, despite the fact that the young man in question took part in the uprising because of the unfair treatment meted out to his subordinates from senior officers.

Keyword CIRCUMSTANCE

Element Air   *Planet* Mercury

Degree 15

It would be difficult for anyone not in possession of the facts to believe that a creature as ugly as a caterpillar could, in the fullness of time, be transformed into the beauty that is a butterfly.

Keyword METAMORPHOSIS

Element Air   *Planet* Mercury

Degree 16

When a confidence trickster finds himself subjected to a similar situation to that which he himself practices daily, he is faced with an irreconcilable dilemma. He cannot seek the assistance of the police to try and recover money to which he had no right in the first place.

Keyword PARADOX

Element Air

Planet Mercury

Degree 17

The duck-billed platypus is indeed possessed of a bill and, like a duck, reproduces by laying eggs. The creature is not a bird and although it suckles its young, neither is it a mammal. For all its peculiarities the creature has flourished for tens of thousands of years, cocking a snoop at orthodoxy.

Keyword DIFFERENCE

Element Air

Planet Mercury

Degree 18

An amateur radio operator picks up a distress signal generated half a world away. Because of his prompt action the crew of a large cargo vessel are saved from perishing with their stricken ship. The sailors will always be grateful to the attentive listener, whose hobby has been the means of their survival.

Keyword UNEXPECTED

Element Air

Planet Mercury

Degree 19

A satirical and cutting political journalist decides to take a more direct part in politics. Eventually he achieves a high rank in the governing party of his country and suddenly finds himself subjected to the same scathing criticism he meted out to others years before.

Keyword RETURN

Element Air   *Planet* Mercury

Degree 20

It is a fact that couples parted by war or national borders, who can see but not speak to each other, are quite capable of communicating telepathically. Such an ability eludes the understanding of science, though there are many aspects of love that cannot be logically explained.

Keyword MYSTERY

Element Air   *Planet* Mercury

Degree 21

Aware of the vast distances between the stars that she or he studies every day, any astronomer knows that at least some of the points of light that filter in through the telescope may have already ceased to exist. Such is the time taken for the light from distant stars the reach to Earth that the astronomer observes time as surely as she or he does distance.

Keyword DEFINITION

Element Air   *Planet* Venus

Degree 22

By dressing and behaving in as unconventional a way as possible, we may consider that we are seeking individuality, a recognition of our uniqueness. If others copy our behaviour we no longer stand out from the crowd, but are we any the less individual?

Keyword INNER-KNOWLEDGE

Element Air   *Planet* Venus

Degree 23

Visitors to a zoo consider themselves to be viewing animals that are typical of their species. Nothing could be further from the truth. Only when in a natural habitat can any creature behave in the way that nature demands for its assured survival. The zoo is an artificial environment.

Keyword RECOGNITION

Element Air   *Planet* Venus

Degree 24

Strolling from street to street the bedraggled and wretched tramp is shunned, but at the same time pitied, by most of the people who see her. Eating and sleeping where she can, she is content that her life should be as it is, for though few realise the fact, she is living the life that she herself chose.

Keyword ATTITUDE

Element Air   *Planet* Venus

Degree 25

Despite many possible explanations, theories concerning the force of magnetism remain just that - theories. Whatever the cause, pieces of magnetised metal cling to each other tightly. However, if placed with identical poles pointing together, instead of seeking to attract, the magnets actively repel their erstwhile embrace.

Keyword OPPOSITES

Element Air   *Planet* Venus

Degree 26

Human experience decrees that violent means must have violent ends. Extremists sometimes believe that moderation should be ignored and that violent behaviour can short circuit the procedure towards meaningful change. All too often the only end achieved is that of the extremists themselves.

Keyword PROGRESSION

Element Air   *Planet* Venus

Degree 27

Out on a coach excursion, a group of visitors are subject to a detour caused by the closure of a road. The travellers are at first somewhat annoyed at this change in their schedule but by the evening they are all forced to admit that the scenery encountered because of the detour was some of the most picturesque they have ever enjoyed.

Keyword ALTERATION

Element Air   *Planet* Venus

Degree 28

A racing driver, up amongst the leaders in a race, uses his intuition in concluding that the weather is about to change for the worse. He loses his position whilst in the pit having wet weather tyres fitted but soon regains it when the rain begins to fall heavily, leaving other drivers unprepared.

Keyword FORETHOUGHT

Element Air   *Planet* Venus

Degree 29

Astrologers are in a unique position, because of their understanding of planetary involvement in human affairs, to advise others on the best course of action to take in times of difficulty. It ought to follow that, possessed of such wisdom, astrologers themselves would never encounter problems in their own lives, but of course they do, frequently.

Keyword FALLIBLE

Element Air   *Planet* Venus

Degree 30

Travelling over hazardous terrain a group of Polar explorers make little headway. Such a permanently frozen and inhospitable wilderness will never be of any practical use to mankind and the laws of common sense would seem therefore to indicate that such an expedition is of no real benefit. The members of the party struggling towards the Pole would not agree.

Keyword ENDEAVOUR

Element Air   *Planet* Venus

♓

PISCES

*The end is the beginning as the timeless
wheel achieves full circle. All endeavour comes to this,
motion without movement. Here and there a part of
the whole appears stark and isolated, but within the
blink of an eye comes to nothing and everything.
At this stage, to the knowing, the purpose,
no purpose becomes
apparent.*

Degree 1

Returning home after an illicit weekend, to a warm welcome from his wife and family, an adulterous husband feels pangs of remorse at his folly. It will take him many weeks to live down his feelings of guilt. For her part, his wife has guessed the circumstances that have taken place and in her heart has already chosen to forgive her husband.

Keyword SELF-INJURY

Element Water   *Planet* Neptune

Degree 2

Having assisted a burglar in several crimes, an accomplice, when brought to justice, is surprised to receive the same sentence as the man who actually committed the offences. The judge explains that since the burglar could not have taken the chances he did without a lookout, the accomplice who performed this task was equally guilty.

Keyword CONDONING

Element Water   *Planet* Neptune

Degree 3

In his desperate struggle to obtain drugs, an addict is driven to acts which normally he would consider abhorrent and horrific. Despite his inability to justify these occurrences morally, he is swayed by his need for the drugs.

Keyword COMPULSION

Element Water   *Planet* Neptune

Degree 4

Supported by a local dignitary to whom he owes his living, an Alchemist spends many hours in his laboratory, seeking to create the philosopher's stone, which he hopes will turn base metals into gold. He will never find his elusive stone but he might make discoveries of other kinds on the way, albeit by accident.

Keyword SEARCH

Element Water   *Planet* Neptune

Degree 5

Early each morning on most beaches, small groups of people can be seen, intently surveying the wealth of treasure left by the receding tide. Very rarely does the sea yield objects of any real financial worth but just occasionally the beachcomber can expect the timeless ocean to yield an odd treasure of significant value.

Keyword OCCURRENCE

Element Water   *Planet* Neptune

Degree 6

Little apparent activity is visible in the sleeper whose only body movement is rapid fluttering of the eyelids. Subconsciously she is involved in adventures never fully experienced by the waking mind, for in addition to the running and swimming possible in everyday life, the dreamer can even fly.

Keyword FANTASY

Element Water   *Planet* Neptune

Degree 7

So besotted is a young man with a woman he has met recently that, despite the knowledge of her previous wickedness and deceit, he is prepared to risk all for her sake. The regard he feels renders him vulnerable for he does not love moderately, a fact that numbs his common sense.

Keyword VALUATION

Element Water   *Planet* Neptune

Degree 8

A well known Medium is caught cheating at a seance by a psychic investigator and is immediately laid open to ridicule by the newspapers. There is no reason to believe that she has cheated before and many individuals swear by her powers despite the adverse publicity. On occasions she can still perform wonders, but nevertheless her reputation is gone.

Keyword FAULT

Element Water   *Planet* Neptune

Degree 9

Whilst travelling in the West Country of England, a motorist on holiday is advised that he must stop at a certain bridge and ask permission of the fairies, who locals say own the bridge, to cross. The motorist laughs for he does not believe in fairies. All the same, upon arriving at the bridge he does take the tale at face value and asks.

Keyword PRECAUTION

Element Water   *Planet* Neptune

Degree 10

Under the effects of a hallucinatory drug, a scientist partaking in an experiment is subject to a series of visions relating to his own research. The information received puts the scientist's endeavours forward by months in a few short hours.

Keyword CONSCIOUSNESS

Element Water   *Planet* Neptune

Degree 11

In former times the existence of mermaids was never disputed by superstitious sailors who knew that the sight of such a creature, at their departure from shore, was the certain harbinger of a shipwreck. Mermaids, they believed, were beautiful creatures to behold but must certainly be considered malevolent.

Keyword CAUTION

Element Water   *Planet* Moon

Degree 12

Being naive concerning the ways of the world, a farmer's son is tricked into parting with all his money in a gambling session. The money is the return from livestock so the youth is loath to return home without it. So long does he tarry, that when he eventually does return home, his parents are so pleased to discover he is safe and well that all thoughts of the money are banished from their minds.

Keyword PRIORITY

Element Water   *Planet* Moon

Degree 13

When a nudist camp is opened at a certain holiday resort the locals are at first outraged. Their protests are to no avail and in any case their attitudes soon alter. Quite apart from the money spent by the nudists themselves, much extra revenue is brought into the town by would-be sightseers.

Keyword POSSIBILITIES

Element Water   *Planet* Moon

Degree 14

A Greek ruler is about to undertake a long journey, in order to enlist the assistance of a famous Oracle, who he hopes will assist him in sorting out a governmental problem. Before he has a chance to depart, the monarch receives a messenger from the Oracle laying out the answer to the difficulty, despite the question never actually being asked.

Keyword UNDERSTANDING

Element Water   *Planet* Moon

Degree 15

Continually being subjected to false alarms, employees of a company are used to hearing the fire siren and they eventually take no notice of it whatsoever. When a genuine fire does break out the management have great difficulty clearing the building, since no-one believes the emergency to be real.

Keyword VIGILANCE

Element Water   *Planet* Moon

Degree 16

In the heat of a midsummer's day, the water of a picturesque canal look cool and inviting. Walkers passing by are enticed to the water, for the sun's glare on its surface prevents them from seeing the jagged metal and broken glass beneath the surface.

Keyword FORETHOUGHT

Element Water   *Planet* Moon

Degree 17

A lone swimmer intends to swim a wide sea channel, aware of the distance but convinced that he is capable of covering the number of miles involved. After further investigations he soon comes to realise that because of winds and tides, the distance to cover will probably turn out to be twice that which is actually shown on the map.

Keyword REALITY

Element Water   *Planet* Moon

Degree 18

When a novelist undertakes a work depicting the future, unless he is possessed of clairvoyant powers, his assessment of that future can only be based on a combination of present understanding and supposition. Much of his book may prove to be inaccurate since human beings do not always act in a logical manner and even nature itself can throw up some surprising twists.

Keyword CONJECTURE

Element Water   *Planet* Moon

Degree 19

Distilling illegal alcohol in a State where its consumption is a serious offence, a distiller could face heavy penalties for his illicit trade. He risks the wrath of the law because of the high profits to be made from a commodity that none are allowed yet which all appear to want.

Keyword DESIRE

Element Water   *Planet* Moon

Degree 20

Having spent a lifetime in study and self-denial, a respected and revered guru is well aware that possibly less than one percent of his students will ever achieve the spiritual awareness that he claims to be attainable. He knows that all his students will benefit in some way however and in any case, one percent of one percent achieving enlightenment would make his teaching worthwhile.

Keyword PURPOSE

Element Water   *Planet* Moon

Degree 21

Having the opportunity of choosing her future career between two schools, one well disciplined and the other chaotic, a prospective headmistress considers carefully. In the end she chooses the post in the hitherto badly run school since she reasons that even anarchy can on occasions form a good basis for lasting stability if she can achieve the respect and goodwill of the pupils.

Keyword CHOICE

Element Water   *Planet* Mars

Degree 22

A fabulously rich potentate spends much of his early life exploring debauchery, vice and low living. Becoming bored, he eventually turns to a totally ascetic life of self-imposed deprivation. Settling into his later years he finally manages to achieve the middle path that he now knows to be true wisdom.

Keyword REALISATION

Element Water   *Planet* Mars

Degree 23

An alcoholic is capable of using, to destroy herself, a commodity which is not in itself evil, since like all things natural alcohol is a gift from God. It is not the liquor that captivates the unfortunate individual but her immoderate use of the substance.

Keyword MODERATION

Element Water   *Planet* Mars

Degree 24

Judging by statues still available for scrutiny in museums, the priestesses of the cult of Vesta in ancient Rome were often incredibly beautiful. Indeed they were partly chosen for the post because of their looks. All worshippers could admire the vestal virgins but none were allowed to touch women who must have seemed as remote as their cold marble statues do today.

Keyword UNAPPROACHABLE

Element Water   *Planet* Mars

Degree 25

Wild ducks are extremely cautious, especially of man, who they recognise as a natural enemy. Despite their reserve, if they observe even badly made decoys floating on the edge of a lake or stream, they will invariably land. The ducks' desire to flock overcomes their fear, even of the voracious hunter, man.

Keyword INSTINCT

Element Water   *Planet* Mars

Degree 26

Looking out from the inside of their aquarium, fishes survey the creatures beyond the extent of their watery world. Every so often these same creatures distribute food on the water or clean the sides and the bottom of the tank. Since the fish were all born in the aquarium, all these strange occurrences are simply an accepted part of their daily life.

Keyword NORMALITY

Element Water   *Planet* Mars

Degree 27

Far out to sea a fishing boat struggles against the prevailing wind and tide. The ferocity of such weather would prove alarming to anyone unused to the sea, but the storm tossed fishermen sit below decks, joking and playing cards.

Keyword EXPERIENCE

Element Water   *Planet* Mars

Degree 28

On the wind swept deck of an ocean based oil rig, men struggle with machinery cold enough to burn the skin from their chilled fingers. Far below them the thick black oil lies waiting, a remnant of the days when this geographical location was a verdant tropical paradise

Keyword TIME

Element Water   *Planet* Mars

Degree 29

Ignoring the niceties of civilised warfare, a General instructs his army to attack the camp of his enemy on the night prior to an intended battle. So surprised are his foe that they surrender with little bloodshed. By his actions the General may have saved thousands of lives, yet, even by his fellow officers, he is branded a coward and a cheat.

Keyword APPEARANCE

Element Water   *Planet* Mars

Degree 30

Far out in the unchartable depths of endless space a small sphere of rock spins in its allotted orbit. This rock is not distinctive, in fact it is quite ordinary and yet to the poor trapped creatures that cling tenaciously to its surface it is everything. The highest life form that peoples the planet is on the verge of interstellar space flight, but no matter where they travel, this grain of sand on the shore of eternity will always be their home.

Keyword RETURN

Element Water   *Planet* Mars

SUN

The Sun is fiery, hot and combative. Oracle responses bound to the Sun by sign or decan must always be viewed in the most dynamic aspect of their interpretation. The Sun is the natural ruler of Leo, the sign of the Lion and wherever the Sun's influence falls, even in other Zodiac Signs, some of the happy, fearless quality of the Lion is present.

Whatever the answer you receive, there will be a desire for practicality in your approach to the response, though it should also be borne in mind that the Sun, through Leo, is ruler of the heart. The result means a degree of emotional consideration that one would more commonly associate with the Moon. Here there may be a difficulty; to respond solely with the head or to accept the more subtle messages that come from the heart.

Read the response again, but this time leave discrimination behind, stand aside from the answer and allow it to filter through at its own pace.

Once you have assimilated the information that you have called through your own needs from the Oracle, accepting its truth with your heart, then you can commence to put it into practice with your head, exemplifying the 'Middle Path' that stands at the centre of so many religions and philosophies.

MOON

The Moon represents one of the least understandable spheres of influence within astrology, hardly surprising when the phases and complicated motions of our nearest neighbour in space are considered.

The Moon rules all emotional reactions, so it is hardly surprising if you are looking for the answer to a problem or situation which speaks more of your inner being than it owes to the world at large. The Moon rules the stomach, hence the 'gut reaction' that is so symptomatic of the seeker's reaction to the Lunar presence. It is highly likely that any other form of action would appear to be inappropriate, either to the initial question, or with regard to the response you have drawn.

But beware, the Moon twists and turns, waxes and wanes, and is rarely likely to elicit the same reaction two days running. Perhaps it would be sensible to sit on your enquiry for a few days, if such is possible. Once you have done so, return to the Oracle; the response might be very similar, though you may not be so responsive to the capricious and inconstant Moon as you could be at present!

MERCURY

Little Mercury, fastest of all the planets, quickest to bring an instant decision but not always the right one in a long term sense.

No planetary influence is either good or bad, all are neutral and everything depends entirely on the way that subtle vibrations are received and utilised. Never is this more true than with Mercury, and though the Oracle can assist you in your quest it cannot live your life for you. In the end the answers are yours to understand.

Mercury is quicksilver, liquid metal, a lightning quick response that will, on occasions, show brilliance in its subtle understanding of the erstwhile unfathomable mysteries of life. With Mercury present, the intellect is vitally important to your understanding of the Oracle's advice. Emotional responses are less likely to be of assistance in this case than they would prove to be with the Moon in attendance.

Look for a flash, an instant and unquenchable spark that you are quite certain represents your answer. In all probability this burst of inspiration was your immediate reaction to the Oracle's advice. If so, look no further. If not, re-phrase your question and look again.

VENUS

Venus is cool and haughty but beautiful and often quite specific. Still there is an enigmatic mystery that leaves the enquirer puzzled for some time and the process is more one of steady filtering than instant understanding.

Venus is the fountain of creativity so it would be hardly surprising if you discover that there is a certain amount of work to done in the building of the solution that eventually becomes clear to you. But it will not be toil for the hammer or the pick, more a subtle and steady remodelling that shapes and contours aspects of your life far beyond the apparent limits of your original question.

Patience is endemic here, not only necessary but readily available, even to the individual who normally would possess none. The Oracle has spoken, so that whether you are instantly in possession of the solution you desire or not, to look again would undoubtedly bring you back, either to Venus or to one of its cool and calculating companions in space.

Do you accept the response of the Oracle? If not there is every possibility that you have failed to understand what, in your subconscious depths, you already know only too well.

Mars

Red, brooding, hot and decisive. So the ancients saw the red planet Mars. Rarely will you have to search deeply, either within the words, or inside yourself, to make sense of the Oracle's responses that fall under the influence of the most immediate and positive planet in space.

But are you guided to Mars because positivity is what you genuinely need, or merely because it is so much a part of your basic nature that you cannot stretch credibility any further? Only you can decide.

There is nothing at all wrong with being positive and decisive, indeed it is one of evolution's most useful bequests to any creature. Sensitivity does not preclude the right or ability to make an instant decision, or to stick to it. Only be certain that your actions do not take you further than the confines of your immediate requirements, for prolonged use of force for its own sake can only lead to karmic retribution.

Mars is the ruler of deep Scorpio, in addition to the more superficial and fiery sign of Aries; either can show through in the various decans that are ruled or sub-ruled by Mars. This may go some way towards explaining the duality that can be represented by the responses under the rulership.

Even though you know that you have to adopt a particular path you could well discover that your decisions are not as popular with others as you might have hoped.

JUPITER

Largest of the planets and known to the ancients as the King of the Gods, the overall importance of Jupiter to the stability and wellbeing of the Solar System is only now becoming clear. Jupiter is expansive and joyful, it can lead you to your desired answers as much through an innate sense of happiness as through any deep sifting of your mental processes.

Jupiter is very large, as may well have to be the overview you take of the various responses that fall within its influence. The longer you consider them, the more far reaching their implications will become. Following the twists and turns of a long, long corridor, the answer to the simplest request could well lead you to a much more fundamental understanding of your own actions and nature.

Although you must take all the responses of the Oracle seriously there is often an element of humour involved where Jupiter is present. Riddles abound and there is invariably more than one way to see a truth or a complex intermixing of truths apparent within the Oracle's advice.

Be generous with the world and in return it will bestow its riches upon you, no matter how perplexed or troubled you may feel yourself to be at this moment in time. The fact that you are led, or lead yourself, to Jupiter, could mean that your problem is almost solved.

SATURN

Saturn has come down to us in many guises, though probably the best known to modern day man is that of Old Father Time. Astrologers from many civilisations have equated the ringed planet with the passing of time. The main inference here is that you will have to give the answers you have achieved time to mature, not only in your mind but also in reality. Saturn rules Capricorn, the sign of the goat, an animal that always achieves its objective, no matter how difficult the obstacles that are thrown in its path. So it is with your question, even if the answers you receive might not be too easy to understand right now.

Confidence might be lacking in your life at present but you do not lack the ability to look forward and build upon a foundation that appears to be little more than an illusion at present. Create the circumstances necessary to allow the answers you seek to mature and then the response that you have drawn from the Oracle will become ever more clear.

Saturn helps you to discover yourself and to grow into a new and more fulfilled life. But beware, there often isn't much humour around with Saturn, even from the Oracle. You will have to provide that for yourself.

URANUS

Uranus was not known to our distant ancestors, only having been discovered in the 18th century, so it isn't surprising that its rulership is geared towards new thought, technology and the like. Revolutions can take place under the auspices of Uranus and that is why so many of the responses that it protects in the Oracle demand a very radical form of action.

Uranus rules the eleventh sign of the zodiac, Aquarius, though it is reflected in other air signs. Aquarius is the age that the world is now entering, a time when convention is overthrown and a breeze of fresh, new thought blows through many spheres of man's existence on the Earth.

The answer that you seek is no less revolutionary in its implications, even if it takes a while for you to understand how to go about turning your world upside down. Don't run away with the idea that all your preconceptions will have to be abandoned however, for no matter how radical the necessary changes might be, they filter through slowly and steadily. Sometimes you may not recognise that anything has happened at all.

NEPTUNE

Most remote of all the solar system's planets, apart from tiny Pluto, Neptune is the ruler of all mystical and psychic experiences. This means that the planet has a special place in the Oracle, which itself relies on the 'hidden' qualities of our minds to bring our own deepest realisations to the fore.

Elusive and nebulous, Neptune opens up new horizons for humanity and could cause you to realise that the response you draw from the Oracle is trying to convince you that you might be asking the wrong question.

Read carefully, go away from the book, and then read again. Coincidences abound in the vicinity of Neptune and there is a possibility that exactly the same advice this book is offering will be forthcoming from entirely different directions.

Your intuition is the key, so avoid searching for an intellectual response if the Oracle guides you to a decan ruled by Neptune. Look inside yourself and hold the response in your mind without mulling it over. Very soon the lessons it offers will become abundantly clear.

FIRE

First of the four elements, fire represents the birth of the Universe and through it all things became possible.

All consuming fire, most destructive and yet most regenerative of the elements. The Phoenix bird, when the time comes for it to die, is consumed on a funeral pyre which marks its demise and yet at the same time its re-birth.

Fire warms the cold but can also lay waste to the beautiful, it must be treated with the greatest respect. Zodiac signs that fall under the influence of the fire element are bold, courageous, combatative and persevering. That is the path that you must consider now, though there are many ways to display these qualities and not all of them mean making a loud noise or bulldozing your way through problems. Sometimes fire can burn cool!

Sooner or later though, action will be needed, you cannot expect your present difficulties to be rectified without becoming directly involved in the situation yourself. With a little confidence there is nothing you cannot achieve.

The fire may be in your own heart, the all consuming,unquenchable sort that is not obvious to the world at large but can be very destructive to you personally. If so, the truths that you draw from the Oracle will show you how to balance the elements in yourself, finding your own peace and bringing calm to all those you meet.

EARTH

The good earth brings forth, in its own time, everything that nourishes and brightens the world. Without the earth nothing can grow, for through its intercedence nature passes from the sterility of fire to the nutrition that all living things require.

Your spirit lives, every bit as much as does your body, and in its own way also requires the solid dependable quality that is the earth element.

The earth moves slowly, waiting for the appointed season, watching and listening. Through its support the humblest seedling can move a mighty boulder or tear up a solid concrete road. How? because it has never been told that such an occurance is impossible and also because with patience anything can be achieved.

If you have already waited a long time for your hopes to become reality, but are certain that what you seek is right and good, take heart from the earth element which guides you now. Soon, all you are looking for can come to pass. But remember, life is full of paradoxes and coincidences. Things will work out, though not necessarily in quite the way you have been expecting.

AIR

Have you ever looked at an eagle, wheeling and soaring high above some mountain peak and wondered at the sheer majesty of flight? It is air that fills out the bird's wings. Invisible but present, yielding yet all powerful. Impossible to live without and yet enigmatic.

Air is the unfathomable, the apparent nothing from which even fire derives its sustenance. In Astrological terms it is the intellect and the air signs buzz with the vibrancy that reflect the 'Prana' of Eastern mysticism. To you at this moment, it is the assurance that you have the intelligence and the knowledge to derive benefit from the responses of the Oracle.

Answers often come quickly and with startling clarity where air is present. Air is the gentle breeze of Spring and the thundering gale of Winter so that its intensity must be monitored and channelled wisely. Its only inherent fault is to be impetuous and thus cause you to misread responses in your desire to turn the world upside down immediately.

Walk wisely and with dignity, do not fight the wind that blows into your face but lean on it, draw strength and wait to observe where it seeks to take you. Your present and future motivation is important, but not more so than your constancy and strength. All is balance.

WATER

From a sparkling, bubbling stream to the deep and rolling ocean, water in its many guises covers the majority of the surface of our planet. Your own body is mainly composed of water and inside you it is altered and replenished, as it is everywhere.

Astrologically, water represents your emotions and psychic potential, these qualities reflecting the vacillating nature of the element. It is hard to hold water and just as difficult to tie down a whim or an intuitional response, yet a great percentage of your life is composed of precisely these feelings.

Of all the elements, water is perhaps the most difficult to understand, and this is reflected in the responses that comprise the Cancer, Scorpio and Piscean sections of the Oracle. Your answers may come drifting ashore on a gentle swell or crashing in on a tidal wave of sudden realisation, never the less, the motivation required to put them into practice is through flexibility and intuition, never through brute force or fixed attitudes.

Love, most powerful of all emotions, is never far from the water element, as difficult to capture as the substance itself and just as refreshing and vital to our wellbeing. Somewhere in your subconscious you will discover that here, more than in any other human expression, the solutions you require can be discovered. Love is the principle that underpins all of creation and it has more power than even the watery depths from where it springs.